Death with
Style and Grace

Death with Style and Grace

VIRGIL L BRADY

iUniverse LLC
Bloomington

Death with Style and Grace

iUniverse books may be ordered through booksellers or by contacting:

iUniverse LLC
1663 Liberty Drive
Bloomington, IN 47403
www.iuniverse.com
1-800-Authors (1-800-288-4677)

ISBN: 978-1-4759-9707-1 (sc)
ISBN: 978-1-4759-9708-8 (ebk)

Printed in the United States of America

iUniverse rev. date: 07/05/2013

CONTENTS

INTRODUCTION

I think about death more than I want. Maybe if I write about my death anxiety, it will diminish. You may ask, "Has it helped?"

Several years ago my son asked, "Are you going to write another book?" I responded, "Actually I have started another book." "What is it about?", asked my son. "Death," I replied. My son looked a little shocked and said, "Why would you write about death? People don't like to think about death. I doubt if you sell many books."

My son is probably right. Therefore, why write a book on how to prepare for death? There are three reasons.

First, throughout my lifetime I was aware of God's call to respond to the hungers and hurts of others. I felt God's presence as I was formulating my words about how to prepare for death.

Second, as a pastor, I received satisfaction through helping people find meaning and purpose in their lives. I had the privilege of being with people at the most important times of their lives. There is no other event in life more important than our own death. I have received satisfaction in thinking I might help people prepare for their death with meaning and purpose.

Third, the literature about death and dying has increased tremendously in recent years. My research, in numerous libraries and the internet, revealed a wealth of material on the topic of death. I discovered that at least 60 percent of the literature deals with death philosophically, theologically and analytically. Another 20 percent centers on a religious approach to death, with emphasis on the afterlife, usually from a fundamentalist Christian viewpoint. The other 20 percent deal with the death of another person. I found surprisingly little written about how to prepare for our own death.

There are, of course, financial and legal ways to prepare, such as establishing a will, durable power of attorney, funeral desires/preferences and a living will. A living will is an advance directive that specifies one's wishes for care in the event of an illness or injury that renders a person unable to speak for himself or herself. An attorney helped me establish these important documents. There are many resources that adequately cover these legal and financial ways of preparing for death. Therefore, I will not address them in this book.

I have come to an amazing and wonderful realization. In the past, I have hovered around an eight on a scale where 10 is the highest amount of death anxiety. By writing, rewriting, reading and rereading this book, my death anxiety has greatly diminished. I now find myself at about a four. I hope reading this book will bring you a similar experience. I would, of course, prefer to be a one or zero, but this is unrealistic, at least for me. Some days, my death anxiety is very low. Yes, there are days when the thought of dying run chills up and down my spine.

It took me over three years to decide on the title for my book. I knew what I wanted to include in the book, but a title that would reveal my purpose eluded me. My son helped me choose the title when he said, "Your title should include the word, grace. That is your word." Indeed, throughout my ministry, grace has been the underlying theme of my sermons. I know that grace (God's unconditional love) is the central theme of the Bible. Grace also refers to a virtue that approaches life experiences, such as death, with elegance, beauty, ease, style and class. I want my death to have style and grace. I hope this book will empower you to live your death with style and grace.

1

PREPARE FOR A
SUCCESSFUL DEATH

"Oh my goodness, I'm going to die." I vividly recall the force of these words the first time I spoke them. I was 25 years old. It was a life changing experience. Oh sure, I knew people died. Prior to this traumatic event, I was aware I would die. However, in this defining moment, the reality of my own death hit me like a ton of bricks. I vividly remember standing outside the church one blistering August afternoon. It was 3:00 p.m.

It was a pivotal moment in my life. A flood of emotions permeated my whole being. The following words express what happened inside me: disturbed, terror, amazed, overwhelmed, futility, dread, empty, hollow, distressed, worried, confused, upset, mad and distressed. It was an unimaginable, weird, inconceivable, and bizarre moment in my life. I felt as if I were slowly sinking under water. A bolt of lightning had struck me. I said, "Maybe I will wake up and realize this is only a dream." The event was surreal. Do you remember the first time you realized you were going to die? Did you have some of these same emotions?

Approximately 150,000 people in the world die every day. This is an interesting statistic. The statistic changes from "interesting" to "devastating" when I realize, I am going to be one of the 150,000.

I don't want to die. You may respond to this statement by saying, "What's new? Nobody wants to die." This, of course, is not true. There are people who want to die and intentionally take steps to end their life. Some people subconsciously enter into self-destructive behavior, which often results in death. Several of my older friends who are in reasonably good health say to me, "I have experienced a lot of living, realize my time is short and I am ready to go."

I recall visiting Sara Louine in the nursing facility of a retirement community. During every visit, she adamantly reminded me how anger engulfs her entire being each morning as she wakes up. She cannot walk. Her hearing and sight are, for all practical purposes, gone. Other parts of her 80-year-old body have deteriorated. Her pain is continuous. Because of physical and/or emotional pain, many people wish they would die.

When I began my thoughts, planning, and research for this book, I was reluctant to let anyone know what I was doing, even my wife. Why? I thought people would think I was weird. Is it morbid to think about death? Eventually, I let the cat out of the bag. "Honey, I am writing a book about death." To my surprise she said, "That's great. This may be your best book." I felt relieved and encouraged. Maybe I'm not so weird or morbid. In fact, I am normal. Many think about death but are simply reluctant to acknowledge it.

Is the Psalmist normal? "Show me, O Lord, my life's end and the number of my days; let me know how fleeting is my life." (Psalm 39:4, New International Version)

My children also helped me feel confident that writing about death was not so weird. My son asked if I were writing another book. "Yes," I said. He continued his inquiry. "What's it about?" I was reluctant to tell him the topic. "Death and dying," I said. "There ought to be lots of people who'd be interested in that subject," he commented. I replied, "I doubt it, but thanks for your encouragement. Your words help me feel thinking about death is normal."

When it comes to dying, I have limited knowledge. I know what it takes to have a fulfilling life. Taking my cue from the Christ event, I spent my professional career proclaiming how to have a meaningful life. Death and dying received little attention in my preaching.

Why would I write about a subject where my knowledge is limited and speculative? The answer has to do with preparation. If we want an event of life to be successful and fulfilling, we will devote a considerable amount of time and energy in preparation.

I invite you to make a list of the three most important events in your life. Before reading the next paragraph, pause and reflect on how preparing for the event was essential in order for it to turn out enjoyable and/or successful.

Is death on your list of important events? Heading up my list are the birth of our children and my wedding. Death always makes my list of the top three most important events of my life.

Think about an event in your life, past or future. It may be a graduation, birth of a baby, marriage, a new job, retirement or . . . Think about the consequences if you do not prepare for the event. Reflect on the positive results that transpire because you prepared. Preparing for an important event in life, such as death, is an intelligent decision.

If we want to perform well in a sport, hobby or skill, preparation increases the chances for success. If you are having surgery you, of course, want it to be successful. Consequently, you expect that your surgeon has prepared extensively for this most important event in your life.

I recall how my college coach, Ralph Miller, prepared us for an upcoming game. Along with the staff, our coach carefully scouted our next opponent. Our squad would watch films of that particular team. At practice, the starting five would scrimmage against our reserve players. The coach schooled the second team on the plays of the opponent. I recall playing the number one team in the nation who had the best player in college basketball, Oscar Robertson. Ralph put a red shirt on a teammate who would represent Robertson. This was the technique used so we would know where he was at all times. This helped us recognize when we were to double-team him and block him out from getting the rebound. Practice included a lot of preparation for the team we were going to play. Preparation was a key to being successful. This is true for any important event, such as death.

The newscast and sirens tell us a tornado may be coming our way. We do not wait until the storm hits our house before we begin to prepare. In Kansas, it makes sense for the city to install a siren system and for people to build houses with basements. An intelligent decision is to prepare for the tornado as a way of insuring it does not overwhelm or destroy us.

What event in life is more important than our own death, and yet most of us have done little to prepare for it. It is an intelligent decision to prepare for our death so our anxiety does not overwhelm and destroy us.

Ian Fleming was an English author, best known for his James Bond series of spy novels. In his eleventh novel, *Only Live Twice*, he writes; "You only live twice: once when you are born and once when you look death in the face."

I would add the word "prepare" to Flemings statement. It is one thing to face death and quite another to prepare for it. You only go around twice: once when you are born and once when you look death in the face and prepare for it.

The discipline of being equipped and ready to meet every event of life has been emphasized with the familiar Boy Scout motto: Be prepared. The great German poet Rilke said, "Death is terrible only for those who are not prepared for it." The sixteenth-century Frenchman Michel de Montaigne wrote, "Death is easiest for those who during their lives have given it most thought as though always to be prepared for its imminence."

Arnold Toynbee wrote, "I can also be certain that death is not going to take me by surprise as an event that has not been in my mind till it has overtaken me." (*Man's Concern with Death*, p. 264)

I wish I knew what my thoughts/feelings would be when I face death directly and immediately. I draw a degree of comfort when I realize, through diligent preparation, I can choose how to respond to the reality of dying.

If you want to play the piano or learn a sport, preparing for such an activity includes having a good teacher. Death can be an invaluable teacher. Preparing for death teaches us how to die and lowers our death anxiety.

Psalm 90:12: "So teach us to number our days aright, that we may gain a heart of wisdom." (New International Version) "Teach us to realize the brevity of life, so that we may grow in wisdom." (New Living Translation) "Teach us to count our days that we may gain a wise heart." (New Revised Standard Version)

On his deathbed, Socrates reportedly made the comment that practicing dying is the highest form of wisdom.

I do not want to miss any part of life that can teach me how to live to the fullest. I am writing this book because I believe death can teach me how to live. Numerous parts of life serve as a teacher, such as books, nature, loving people, music, art, babies and religion. Using death to teach us how to live is a wise decision.

In an interesting way, I have already prepared for death. I draw comfort and strength from knowing I have had to deal with several death experiences throughout my lifetime. The death of my parents was my first encounter with death. Yes, I could never fully prepare for their dying. I cried each time my children left home for college. It was a death experience. Moving to another town was a death experience.

I recall being in the locker room of North Texas State University. I just concluded the final game of my college basketball carrier. I realized I would never again put on a basketball uniform and play the game I loved. This was a significant death experience. Even retirement was a death experience. My life as a full-time pastor was over.

When I think about these death experiences, I realize I was able to adjust and move on with my life. This realization gives me comfort and strength. I feel encouraged. Maybe I can approach death with the same degree of inner strength. Yes, in a significant way, these death experiences are different from physical death. Nevertheless, how we deal with the many death experiences of life gives us a hint as to how we can deal with death.

Can anyone really prepare for their own death, especially since there are so many unknowns surrounding the event?

Several years ago, Elaine and I planned a three-week trip to Europe. We took the suggestions from those who had gone before; travel light. Our backpacks held everything we needed. We quickly discovered that unforeseen contingencies arose for which we were not prepared.

Because of our preparation, the unforeseen events did not completely ruin the experience. We were able to adjust.

Unforeseen contingencies will continually affect life's journey. Being prepared enables us to adjust to the reality that some day we will die. Our death anxiety will not ruin the experiences of life when we have prepared.

In hindsight, it was impossible to prepare for all the unforeseen events of our European trip. They just happened. Can anyone completely prepare, given the fact each of us could die instantly and without warning? Can anyone fully prepare for lying in a casket or, in the case of cremation, have our body completely burned to ashes? I have been with parents as they viewed their newborn baby in a casket. I have held the hand of numerous persons while they were in process of dying. Can a person really prepare for such an event?

Preparing for an event we know is going to happen is different from preparing for an unknown event. One of the most unsettling aspects of death is the unknown. Preparing for death helps a person deal with fear of the unknown.

About 20 years ago, Elaine and I were on our morning jog. In untypical fashion, Elaine lagged behind. She always jogged faster and farther. After a week, I confronted her. "What is going on?" I asked. "I just haven't gotten over my flu episode several months ago," she replied. After several weeks of what I perceived to be denial, I insisted she see a doctor. The hospital conducted a series of tests. Late in the afternoon, the doctor phoned with the test results. She had leukemia. The doctor said he did not know what kind of leukemia and referred us to a specialist in Kansas City.

We were, of course, devastated. We knew little about leukemia except that it was serious. We began reading about it and sought information from our doctor friends. We discovered there is acute and chronic leukemia. Acute is fast acting and can result in a quick death. Chronic leukemia comes in many varieties. We had to wait four days before we could see the specialist. The unknown was killing us. Even though the news was shocking, knowing the name of her kind of leukemia was better than staying stuck in the unknown. We were still afraid, but the fear lessened when we heard the name, *hairy cell* leukemia.

It was the chronic form. Correct information lessened the fear of the unknown.

There are many unknown aspects of death. Fear of the unknown is normal and expected. Fear becomes less intense when the unknown becomes known. The knowledge and awareness that accompanies being prepared lowers the degree of anxiety.

When I think of myself reduced to ashes, an eerie feeling emerges. I often wonder why feelings of depression and futility do not accompany my eerie feeling. I contribute it to the preparation I have done in learning how to live and die in the light of God's grace. The ideas in this book are helping me prepare.

Preparing for your own death is neither weird nor morbid. It is an intelligent decision. I trust preparing for death will free you from either avoiding your death anxiety or being consumed by it.

I hoped writing about death would get rid of my death anxiety. Likewise, I wanted each book on death that I read to eliminate my death anxiety. This did not happen. If you have picked up this book with the same hope, you will be disappointed. My degree of death anxiety has not completely disappeared. It has significantly decreased. I feel a sense of freedom when I accept the fact that I will always have a degree of anxiety.

In my research for this book, I came across several books with the title, *The Art of Dying*. Indeed preparing for death is an art. "Art" is defined as, "the process of creating a beautiful and significant skill or craft, a finer skill that can be learned by study, practice and observation." Socrates stated that philosophy is practicing the art of dying.

As is true with drawing, writing, playing a musical instrument or developing a craft/trade, dying is an art. Study, practice and observation develop the art of dying. The following chapters will help you develop the art of preparing to die.

If I am the only person who reads this book, my writing will not be in vain. Putting these ideas on paper has been therapeutic to me in my "golden" years. I hope the same will happen for you as you prepare for death.

People frequently ask, "What should I say to a friend who has experienced the death of a loved one?" How can we adequately answer this question unless we have prepared for our own death? I have witnessed how people, wanting to be helpful to someone in grief, say and do unhelpful things. They have not sufficiently prepared for their own death. Dealing with our own death anxiety increases our chances of being helpful to others at their time of death.

I am sad when I think of the millions upon millions of people whose life ended prematurely, who experienced a senseless death and did not have the opportunity to prepare for dying. I feel fortunate to have the opportunity to prepare for my death. I trust you consider yourself fortunate to have the opportunity to prepare for the most important event of your life.

Maxine admitted her mother to the hospital. She called to tell me the bad news. Her mother had about two weeks to live. Maxine wanted me to visit her mother. As I drove to hospital, I contemplated what I would say. Would I say, "I hear you have only two weeks to live?" This sounded too abrupt. Would I avoid the news and see if she brings up the topic?

When I walked into the hospital room, Maxine's mother was sitting up. I said, "Hi, Millie." "Hi pastor." I gave her my opening words; "Your daughter called and told me you were in the hospital. How are you doing?" Millie was very perceptive. She could sense I knew the answer to my question and was somewhat uncomfortable talking to someone who had only two weeks to live. I remember distinctly her exact words. She said, "I have not left this matter until this hour." As I pondered her comment, Millie conveyed how, throughout her life, she had spent some time preparing for her death. She was at peace. People such as Millie helped me write this book on how to prepare for death.

I invite you to join me in preparing for death rather than leaving this matter until the hour comes. If you want to find meaning and purpose in your life, preparing for death is a crucial part of that quest.

When I was in college, I lived in a large dormitory. Each year as we arrived for the new semester, we were required to review the "exit strategy." The dorm authorities wanted to make certain we were informed on what to do in case of fire. The purpose of the exit strategy was to prevent unnecessary problems, to ourselves and others. The exit strategy prepared us for responsible action. We never knew if or when a fire would occur, but we were adequately prepared. The exit strategy laid out a clear road map so we could respond in a way that made sense. The exit strategy minimized the chances of being devastated by a fire. The exit strategy provided personal relief and assurance in the face of what might happened in the unforeseen future.

I hope the following chapters will be a helpful and informed exit strategy as you face the unknown future. The purpose of preparing for death is to prevent unnecessary problems to yourself and others that often happen when thoughts of dying arise. We never know when the exit will happen; nevertheless, we can be adequately and responsibly prepared in a way that makes sense. Here is a strategy, a road map, to minimize the chances of being devastated by thoughts of dying. Rather than responding with a high intensity of anxiety, the exit strategy laid out in following chapters will hopefully give personal relief and assurance as you prepare for your exit from this life.

Having an exit strategy for life is a wise and realistic decision. This includes not only financially and legally, but also emotionally and spiritually.

I invite you to join me in looking at how to prepare for death, so your exit will be filled with style and grace.

QUESTIONS FOR CONTEMPLATION AND DISCUSSION

1. What were your thoughts and feelings the first time you realized you were going to die?
2. What positive things can happen because you have spent time preparing to die with style and grace?
3. What death experiences have you had throughout your life and how did you deal with those events?
4. In what way did preparation for a particular important event in your life contribute to making it a positive experience?

2

THE ULTIMATE
BALANCING ACT

A friend asked, "Now that you are retired, what are you doing these days besides playing golf?" "I'm writing a book," I replied, "A book about what?" "I'm writing about how to prepare for death and dying." My friend responded, "That's interesting. Actually, I don't think about death. When my time is up, it's up. You can't do anything about it. It's going to happen, so why waste time worrying about it?" Is my friend facing reality or avoiding his feelings about death?

I recall making a pastoral visit to a man who was dying of cancer. The wife met me at the door and said, "I suggest you not mention dying to my husband. He is trying to focus on maintaining hope and doesn't want to talk about dying." She invited me into the bedroom where her husband was bedfast. I asked the wife if I could visit with him, alone. It was only a few minutes before the husband whispered to me, "You know I am dying, but my wife can't bear to talk about it. It's too painful. She believes there will be a miracle and I won't die." Is this couple facing reality or avoiding their feelings about death?

If walking through a particular door will bring me pain, I am inclined to avoid going through that door. Most of us tend to avoid uncomfortable experiences of life, such as death.

When you are preparing for an important event, is it helpful or not helpful to avoid uncomfortable and painful issues?

11

After seven years of marriage, Mary and John began to realize the ways they were different. For example, Mary was an extrovert and John an introvert. Because of their differences, tension evolved. Should they simply avoid their differences or would avoidance, in the long run, increase the tension.

All of us have heard unhappy stories of someone who could have prevented a debilitating disease if he/she had paid attention to the signals happening in their body. Poor health is frequently the result of avoiding what the body is telling us.

I recall a couple who made some unwise financial decisions. They were moving toward an unstable and uncertain future. Should they avoid examining the nature of those decisions?

Whether it is health, finances, marriage or death, avoidance frequently makes matter worse.

Avoidance is often the way we deal with anxiety, especially death anxiety. Death haunts us like nothing else. Preparing for death begins by facing honestly our tendency to avoid thinking about it.

In earlier years, a person did not have as much time to avoid thinking about death. The accepted assumption is that prehistoric man had an average life expectancy of about 18 years. In this hunter-gatherer phase of human evolution, a lingering death due to old age was rare.

In 1830, only one-third of Americans lived to age 60. By 1900, it was one-half. By 1940, it increased to two-thirds. Today, the number who survives to age 60 is over 80%. The U.S. Census Bureau's predicts the average life expectancy in the United States will be in the mid-80s by 2050, up from 77.85 in 2006.

We are living longer due to organ transplants, respirators, feeding tubes, angioplasty, cardiac and circulatory drugs, and chemotherapy. If I had lived in earlier days, I would have died several times before the age of 40. Appendicitis and gall bladder stones would have killed me without the availability of modern medicine and surgery. My wife would have died in her early forties from cancer.

These marvels of modern medicine afford us more time to prepare for our death. Ironically, we also have more time to experience the negative consequences of avoidance.

Herman Feifel is recognized as a major player in bringing the issue of avoidance to the forefront. His initiative can be traced to the first scientific symposium on death and behavior which was organized and chaired by Feifel in 1956 at the annual meeting of the American Psychological Association in Chicago. Three years later, Feifel wrote *The Meaning of Death*. He inspired people to break entrenched taboos against death and motivated people to make death and dying an important area of inquiry.

The work of Feifel and Elizabeth-Kubler Ross initiated the thanatological transformation. The word *thanatology* is derived from the Greek language. In Greek mythology, thanatos (θάνατος) is the personification of death. Thanatology is a school of thought dedicated to the study of the social and psychological aspects of death. Thanatology, as a professional discipline, gathered momentum following several publications including Feifel's book and *The Psychology of Death* (1972) by Robert Kastenbaum and Ruth Aisenbery.

Feifel's work made the study of death a legitimate subject for scholarly and scientific study. Feifel has been called the father of the modern death movement. Although both Feifel and Kubler-Ross are credited with raising awareness of death and dying, Feifel laid the foundation. By the end of the 1960s, a decade after *"The Meaning of Death"* was published, Kubler-Ross' book, *On Death and Dying*, became popular.

Ernest Becker's Pulitzer Prize winning book, *The Denial of Death,* (1973) has been the reference point for examining the personal and cultural consequences of avoidance. Becker says the primary and overarching motivation for many of our thoughts and action is fear of death. Yearning to live, yet knowing one is destined to die, is posited as a fundamental underlying motivator of human behavior. Becker says fear of death ultimately determines all our actions and experiences as individual beings and as a society. He contends that in our need to triumph over personal mortality, our struggle tends to exacerbate, rather than alleviate the existence of suffering.

Becker points out how, in the face of death, our anxious feelings are the result of feeling helpless. This helpless feeling is so overwhelming that we conspire to keep it unconscious. We avoid. Becker suggests we attempt to safeguard our identity by connecting with what appears to be permanent or enduring. All religions, Becker says, function as "immortality systems" because they promise to connect our lives with a meaning that does not perish.

Extensive studies and research reveal how death, on a conscious and unconscious level, is a fundamental motivation for many of our actions and attitudes. Terror Management Theory (TMT) advocates have led the way on this topic. The writings of Ernest Becker inspired this theory. Social psychologists Jeff Greenberg, Tom Pyszczynski and Sheldon Solomon proposed the Terror Management Theory in 1986.

Numerous studies have explored how death is a motivating factor in a variety of ways and in an assortment of issues. The issues include aggression, stereotyping, need for structure and meaning, driving habits, sex, self-esteem, marriage, fairness, environmental concerns, religion, anxiety management, hate crimes, violence in movies, support for charities, risk taking, decision-making, political identity, attitudes towards women, responses to trauma, materialism and many other issues central to human experience.

Far from facing death, the contemporary mind denies and/or avoids the reality of the person's death. This factor results in a compulsive drive for self-satisfaction, which is causing much of the modern angst.

Robert Neale's book, *The Art of Dying,* refers to an essay by Geoffrey Gorer, *The Pornography of Death.* They contend that our society represses a healthy acceptance of death in much the same way the Victorian era suppressed sex. In fact, Neale and Gorer assert pornography can be a way of avoiding the deep feelings that are part of a sexual relationship. Attention to death in our culture has become pornographic in nature. We can give attention to death while at the same time avoiding the deep feelings that are present.

While death is before us in the media, we actually distance ourselves from death by the way we portray it in our culture. Gratification comes by avoiding the fears that come as we contemplate our own death.

Therefore, death not only surrounds us, but we search it out. We seek it in order to deny it. Television and movies temper the reality of death, as the experience of death comes into our lives secondhand. We can experience, vicariously and in total safety, dangers that would have caused an immediate personal response in past generations.

Modern media fictionalizes death, weaving the act of dying into a world of fantasy in which the sight of a dead individual has about the same emotional impact as the sight of an advertisement for soap. Pictures on the screen create in the minds of viewers a sense that death, even our own deaths, can be brushed aside as make-believe. The perversions may be sadistic, violent and vile. The fantasies incite fascination that keeps us from dealing forthrightly with our deepest thoughts and feelings about death. This helps explain how people can view a movie that contains violent death and return home feeling they have conquered their fear of death, when, in fact, they have participated in a subtle form of avoidance and denial.

Is avoidance of death as prevalent as some have claimed? For example, death has been a topic of increasing attention in academia and popular literature. The hospice movement has grown. There are many who argue that the American relationship to death and dying is changing. Avoidance and denial seem to coexist with a newly fashioned thrust toward openness. In fact, some would argue we are obsessed with death and it occupies too much attention.

I recently read there are over 1700 books now in print asserting that we are ignoring the subject of death. Newpapers, magazines and TV bombard us with accounts of accidents, homicides, suicides and live pictures of death from the battlefields. Watching the pictures of 911 can hardly be labeled as avoidance. Approximately 70 million people die every year. A glut of information has appeared on the Internet, bringing the subject of death within arm's length. Search the word "death" in your computer and select from more than 23,600,000 items. Hospice advocates and practitioners have heightened the awareness of death and dying.

Most books on the subject of death approach the topic philosophically and analytically. Other books deal with the death of a loved one. However, these books do not adequately address the feelings surrounding our own thoughts of death.

Given all that is happening in our society concerning death, how can anyone seriously suggest we are a death-denying culture? How can anyone really avoid death? There is a big difference between hearing or reading about someone's death and contemplating our own death.

We can become detached and even hardened when we read about other people dying. Attempting to become detached and hardened to the reality of our own death is just that, an attempt.

It is not easy to tell yourself to stop thinking about death. It is like trying to avoid thinking about a pain in your stomach. Preoccupation with something may defer thoughts about pain. However, that "something" is only temporary before returning to thoughts about the pain.

For example, if I waved a hammer in front of your face, could you avoid thinking about the hammer? It would be very difficult, if not impossible. There may be some with the mental discipline to ignore the hammer. There may be some with the mental discipline to avoid thinking about dying. However, if I hit you on the head with the hammer it would be virtually impossible to avoid thinking about the hammer and the pain it has given you.

Death is more than just a thought passing before our eyes. Thoughts and feelings of our own death hit us like a hammer. It is virtually impossible to stop thinking about it.

Some degree of avoidance is inevitable and normal. It is normal for people to try avoiding unpleasant topics. In the face of our own death, without a degree of avoidance, without our defenses, fears would be overwhelming. Protection is necessary and desirable for self-fulfillment. Otherwise, loneliness and separation would overwhelm us. Avoidance is a way of protecting ourselves from the alarm of our death.

Two years ago, I asked my wife if she thinks much about dying. She said, "No, not really. I have more important things to think about." At the time, I asked myself whether her response was her way of coping with death anxiety. Was she avoiding thinking about her death? Two years later, she reports that she thinks a lot more about death. In fact, she was writing down her funeral desires.

My point in sharing this story is this: When thinking about one's own death, people cope in different ways. Two years made a significant difference to my wife.

Some people cope with death anxiety by keeping busy in their work and/or play. Some cope by believing they will continue to live in heaven. Still others avoid thinking about dying with various methods of escape, such as drugs and alcohol. In my judgment, some of the ways people use to cope and handle thoughts of dying are healthy and some are unhealthy. One of my coping mechanisms is to write about it.

Age, state of physical and emotional health, family, social and religious backgrounds, degree of psychological maturity and past experiences with death are all factors that determine how people cope with death anxiety.

There is, of course, the age-old discussion about what influences behavior the most, environmental factors or genetics. The degree to which genetics triggers anxiety varies, depending on which research and theory you read. Some psychoanalysts believe anxiety arises from past fearful experiences. Others scientists link anxiety to a biochemical imbalance in the brain that can be alleviated with the use of medication or natural food supplements. Currently, substantial research is taking place to discover the role of genetics in inducing anxiety.

Laughter is a way some cope with death anxiety. With laughter, we can insulate ourselves from our fears.

Comedian Jerry Seinfield says, "According to most studies, people's number one fear is public speaking. Number two is death. Does that sound right? This means the average person attending a funeral thinks they'd be better off in the casket than doing the eulogy."

Woody Allen says, "I don't mind dying. I just don't want to be there when it happens."

Here are two of my favorite jokes about death.

A wife and her friend took a two-week trip to Europe. The husband was left alone with the mother-in-law and their cat, Fluffy. After a couple of days the cat died. His wife had a deep attachment to Fluffy. After the wife had been gone for a couple days, she called home and asked how things were going. The husband said, "Fluffy died." The wife was distraught and somewhat angry that he had so bluntly told her Fluffy had died. She said, "Why didn't you slowly lead me into this bad news. Why didn't you say, for example, Fluffy is on the roof? Then the next day when I called, you could have said Fluffy fell off the roof and we had to take her to the hospital. The next day when I called, you could tell me she wasn't doing very well in the hospital. The next day, you could have told me Fluffy died, and I would have been prepared for the bad news." The husband said, "I didn't think about that. I was insensitive. I should have done what you have suggested. I'll do that the next time." In a couple days, the wife called again and asked, "How are things going?" He said, "Well, your mother is on the roof."

A man died and went to heaven. Saint Peter met the man at the gate and said he would have a Volkswagen to drive around heaven. Evidently, the type of car you get in heaven depends on the kind of life you live. The man was hoping for a Cadillac or Mercedes. He was clearly disappointed but got into his used VW bug and drove off. About a block down the street, he veered off and crashed into a telephone pole. Saint Peter heard the crash and ran to see how the man was doing, only to find him lying beside the road bleeding and laughing. Saint Peter asked him, "What are you laughing about?" "Well," said the man, "I was disappointed that I got a VW until I saw my preacher go by on a skateboard." (This is a funny story but, of course, bad theology. Our eternal salvation depends upon God's grace rather than how we live our life. The Bible is clear about this truth, and it is the essence of Jesus' ministry and message.)

In light of the fact that a degree of avoidance is necessary and inevitable, while at the same time keeping in mind the negative consequences of avoidance, it is important to acknowledge some positive aspects of avoidance. I am sure you can think of examples. Here are several.

You have been happily married for over 40 years. Twenty years ago, you were at a conference and talking with a member of the opposite sex. One thing led to another and you found yourself taking a drive with that person. You drove to a park where you embraced and kissed. Both of you realized it was not right. You get into the car and return to the conference site. Nothing more happened. Should you avoid telling your spouse of 40 years about this incident? The answer depends upon multiple factors. Avoidance may be a viable option.

You have been married for over 40 years. When you were a sophomore in high school, you got pregnant. You and your parents decided abortion was the best option. Do you tell your spouse of 40 years about this event? Avoidance may or may not be the best option.

Your spouse is seriously ill. You have experienced a painful event at work. Your job is in jeopardy. Should you tell your spouse if it would only make her medical condition worse? If you avoid telling her, would that be the best option?

In face of these and other examples where avoidance appears to be an attractive option, nevertheless, I lean heavily towards facing reality, including our death anxiety. At the same time, I am slow to judge another person's pattern of avoidance. For example, I simply cannot face the stark realities and scenes of the Holocaust without turning my head and ignoring, to some degree, what happened to six million Jews.

Although avoidance is understandable, it is important to acknowledge how avoidance is a major source of unhappiness and fosters dangerous and destructive behavior. We cannot unravel the complexities of human behavior and fully understand others and ourselves without confronting the issues, feelings and thoughts related to death and dying.

Becker makes the point that with denial we do not "get to our authentic self: what we really are without sham, without disguise, without defenses against fear . . . We shrink from being fully alive . . ."

A part of me wishes I could be like those who say they do not worry about dying. The caution I would interject is whether their thoughts and feelings have gone into their subconscious and, in time, will emerge even more toxic and dangerous. Avoidance may work for a time, but it ultimately only leads to complications and problems.

The techniques we have developed to avoid and repress our thoughts and feelings about death ultimately begin to choke us. Self-deception and pretending ultimately leave a person with more problems than facing the reality of our own death.

Avoidance and defense mechanisms are frequently manifested in behavior detrimental to society, our world and ourselves. The following examples are four pathological consequences of the most insidious and unhealthy results of people avoiding death anxiety.

1. Greed

As I write this on October 14, 2011, our country is experiencing what some are calling an economic downfall. The unemployment rate is over double digits in some states. Each political party has a different philosophy when it comes to solving the economy. Meanwhile, hundreds are protesting in the streets of many U.S. cities. Their message: "Greed" is the major reason for the economic turmoil.

Several years ago, the stock market took a drastic tumble. I was visiting with a friend who makes his living helping people invest in the stock market. I asked, "What is going on? What makes the market drop this much in such a short time?" I expected him to give me a short course on economics. I waited for him to expound on the complexities of how money works. Instead, he responded with one word, "greed." In a way, I was surprised. On second thought, his insight confirmed my opinion: greed is a major cause of personal unhappiness and a source of many problems our country is facing.

Obviously, many factors affect the status of our national economy and the stock market. However, greed is one factor that must remain in the conversation. In my research of TMT, numerous articles report how denial of death is a significant factor in people becoming materialistic and greedy.

Thoughts of dying bring feelings of helplessness and insecurity. In our insecurity, we tell ourselves having more money will keep us from worrying about our inevitable demise. Wealth is a symbolic manifestation against death. By building something we think will last, we feel we can gain a degree of control over our helplessness.

In the face of death, people tend to acquire more toys. TMT experiments indicate that after experiencing a mortality-salience induction, persons will increase their materialistic pursuits as a way of avoiding thoughts of dying. The conclusion is that people's tendencies toward materialism and consumption stem in part from a source unlikely to disappear, the fear of death.

The danger of greed is, of course, not a new topic. Many years ago, Jesus spent a considerable amount of time pointing out the perils of greed. For example, he called people "fools" who lay up treasures for themselves. (Luke 12:13-21) "Beware of all covetousness, for a person's life does not consist in the abundance of possessions." (Luke 12:15)

Socrates chastised the Athenians at his trial. "Are you not ashamed that you give your attention to acquiring as much money as possible, and similarly with reputation and honour, and give no attention or thought to truth and understanding and the perfection of your soul? . . . People think the real problem in life is to escape harm and death. But I suggest that the difficulty is not so much to escape death; the real difficulty is to escape from doing wrong." (*Apology*)

In my judgment, greed is more of a threat to our country than terrorism. When it comes to losing our respect throughout the world, greed is a contributing factor. If I am right, it is even more imperative that we prepare for our dying, so our avoidance of death anxiety does not lead to more and more greed.

2. Prejudice

Avoidance of death contributes to prejudice. Prejudice arises from several factors. Nevertheless, we cannot ignore the bulk of literature that reveals how unconscious and conscious concern about death activates prejudice towards those who are different due to race, nationality, religion or sexual orientation.

We feel insecure knowing we are going to die. Out of our insecurity, we will put others down. Feeling we are better than others lowers the level of insecurity.

How do we eliminate prejudice and racism? Many good suggestions have been offered. How death anxiety and prejudice are connected calls for vigilant attention. Rather than spending so much time trying to avoid our death anxiety, preparing for death ensures we are addressing the harmful effects of prejudice.

3. War/violence

In addition to greed and prejudice, the lack of clarity about what motivates people to war will also eventually destroy us, as individuals and as a nation.

We are told war is justified because it is a national security issue. We must go to war if we want to have peace. We must fight wars if the freedoms we enjoy are to continue.

There are, of course, many reasons why we fight wars. These factors include economics, politics, poverty, terrorism, patriotism, greed, prejudice, dictatorships and oppression. I am sure you can add to the list. The inevitability of death also motives us to fight wars. We feel powerless, helpless and vulnerable. War is a way to gain back a degree of power and control over our lives.

When people think about ending up in ashes or a coffin, they often question the meaning of life. Even amidst the unspeakable horrors, war gives what we long for in life. It can give us purpose and meaning, albeit a false sense of purpose and meaning. War is a psychological defense for taming the terror of our mortality. War helps obliterate our fear of death.

It is the old fight or flight dynamic. If you are sitting on a park bench and someone begins to hit and rob you, what will you do? You will either fight or flight. You will not just sit there, receive the pain and do nothing. Likewise, when we experience the pain of death anxiety, the fight or flight response kicks in. War is a ready target for the fight or flight response. We can fight a war, which has risk, intrigue and danger. Fighting a war provides power and purpose in the midst of the helpless feeling associated with death. For some, war helps assure their life is making a difference.

To suggest that unconscious feelings of death motivate people to fight wars is certainly a controversial idea. We have convinced ourselves that war is not our doing, but a response to the evils of others. How easily we demonize the enemy in order to justify our decisions for war.

To be sure, terrorism and the wickedness of others are real. There are evil people in the world. However, if this is only reason we consider when making decisions about going to war, we are setting ourselves up for disaster, personally and as a nation. For many, responding to evil continues to be the only and/or primary reason for war. It is in our national interest for us to acknowledge how our death anxiety drives us to war.

Is there any hope? Will we always be at war with someone? In my judgment, hope comes as we resist the tendency to avoid our thoughts and feelings about death. Hope comes by giving serious consideration and conversation to the fact that the threat of others comes from within as much or more than from without. Will terrorism and a small country with a nuclear bomb destroy us, or will we destroy ourselves by not facing the psychological reasons we go to war? The least we can do is ask this question.

I have written only a few short paragraphs about an issue that is extremely complex and controversial. My brief reflections only superficially touch the issue of what has motivated every nation, in every generation throughout history, to follow the path of war.

Is it naïve and unrealistic to believe there is a better way of responding to terrorism and ruthless dictators? Was Jesus naïve when he said, "Love your enemies? If someone strikes you on one cheek, turn the other cheek?" Was Jesus unrealistic when he said, "Pray for those who persecute you?" Obviously, many humans say they believe in Jesus, but find it naïve and unrealistic to follow his teachings. At least, let us continually raise the question as to how a power other than military power can solve complex international problems. Let us strive to find what William James called the "moral equivalent of war." We can begin by confessing how the tendency to avoid our death anxiety affects our decision-making about who is an enemy and how to deal with an adversary. Preparing for our death is a good place to start.

4. Apotheosis

Apotheosis (from the <u>Greek</u> αποθέωσις, "to deify"; in Latin, *deificatio,* "making divine") is the glorification of a subject to <u>divine</u> level. Apotheosis refers to the idea that an individual has been elevated to the status of a god. In ancient times, historical figures were often worshiped as gods. For example, the emperor Augustus ordered that Julius Caesar be recognized as a god and thus began a tradition of deifying emperors.

For years, I have been interested in how intelligent and loving people could follow Adolph Hitler. How could so many people become part of a cult, such as Jim Jones' People's Temple where 638 adults and 276 children committed suicide for their cause?

23

This kind of blind devotion, deification and adulation of another human being can be traced to how people consciously and subconsciously avoid their death anxiety. In the face of death, people feel powerless. Therefore, they feel a degree of power by giving loyalty to those who appear to have power.

Becker refers to this personality pattern in the familiar Freudian terms of "transference." Because we feel we cannot do much about the power of death, some will endow certain persons with power. Someone is taking care of them. They feel not all is in vain. Amidst the uncertainty of death, this god-like person, on our behalf, now has power to control, order and combat death. In the presence of that individual, some people feel they have found a safe place and control their own fate, even death. It is a way of achieving importance, stability and permanence. This is a way to sidestep honest self-examination, such as facing their thoughts and feelings about death.

Apotheosis makes it all the more important to examine the issue of death avoidance and begin preparing for our death in a forthright and courageous way.

Although avoidance leads to many unnecessary problems, thoughts of death can be overwhelming and paralyzing. Someone has said the human mind is as little capable of contemplating death for any length of time, as the eye is able to look at the sun. If our thoughts of death were continuous, we would not be able to function normally.

Therefore, a full and authentic life comes by finding a healthy and creative balance between being consumed with death thoughts *and* complete avoidance.

When addressing the issue of establishing a balance between avoidance and facing the reality of death, Otto Rank uses the word "partialize". Rank, an Austrian psychoanalyst and close friend of Freud, was a pioneer in existential psychotherapy in the United States. In *Will Therapy* he writes, "Our feelings of anxiety run in opposite directions, one towards separation and individuation; the other towards union and collectivity." Ranks says life is impossible without these two potentially conficting aspects of life. "The well-adjusted person develops the capacity to "partialize" the world for comfortable action. While no one fully accomplishes this balancing act, the more persons are able find this balance the better they will be able to live a genuine fulfilling life."

Rank's word, *illusion*, is helpful in establishing a balance. On what level of illusion does one live? What is the best illusion under which to live? How much freedom, dignity and hope does a given illusion elicit? These three questions absorb the natural neurosis that thoughts of death elicit and open the door for creative living.

Establishing a healthy balance includes the matter of frequency and intensity. Do you frequently think about dying? How intense are your thoughts and emotions? I think about death frequently, at least, it seems frequent to me. However, the intensity of my thoughts and feelings seem manageable. Yes, there are times when the thought of dying hits me like a bolt of lightning. Most of the time my thoughts and feelings about dying are, what I consider, under control. I can live with the intensity. I would prefer to minimize the frequency.

How does one find a balance between being consumed by death anxiety and completely avoiding our feelings and thoughts. How can I restore a sustainable balance between avoidance and an intelligent response to death's reality? Finding and living a balance that fits for your personality is not an easy task; nevertheless, it is an important part of my preparation for death.

The ideas in the following chapters help me establish a balance. I hope reading this book will do the same for you.

QUESTIONS FOR CONTEMPLATION AND DISCUSSION

1. Have you avoided the issue of your own death? Why? Why not?
2. What do you understand to be the consequences of avoiding thoughts of death?
3. How do you respond to the idea that death is a major motivating factor for many of life's issues, such as the economy, prejudice and war?
4. Do you think that in some of life's situations, avoidance is normal and even preferred? Why? Why not?
5. If you established a balance between being consumed by thoughts of death and avoidance, what would that balance look like?

3

IS THIS HOW YOU FEEL?

May Lou is unhappy in her marriage. She tells the counselor that her husband works all the time. "He never has time for me." The counselor asked, "How do you feel when he does this?" She replies, "I feel he is self-centered. His priority is himself and his work." The counselor repeated the question, "And how do you feel about this?" She answers, "I feel he will never change. He has been this way for 20 years." The counselor persisted, knowing it was important for May Lou to identify her feelings. "You have told me what you are thinking. I want to know how you are feeling. Tell me how you feel when you think about him not changing?" "I feel hopeless," May Lou responded.

May Lou readily informed the counselor what she was thinking, but was slow to convey her feelings. People talk about their thoughts, while being reluctant to openly acknowledge and share their feelings, especially if the feelings are painful and deep. This is especially true when it comes to thoughts and feelings about death. People talk *about* death but are hesitant to deal with their feelings. Thinking rationally about death is important. It is more important to understand the feelings we have about death and deal with them in a healthy manner.

There are four basic feelings surrounding our thoughts of death.

I.   Scared/Afraid/Fear

   Dealing with our fear, so it does not consume us, begins by defining the nature of the fear. Here is a list of the most common fears associated with death. You may add to the list a fear that is real for you.

1.   I am afraid of not seeing my loved ones, a sunset, the changing of the seasons or the birth of a grandchild. I feel scared when I reflect on everything I am going to miss.

2.   I am afraid of becoming a burden to my children, wife and others. I do not want to inconvenience others who may have to make medical decisions for me. I know children who have had to change their parent's diapers. You may know children whose parents did not recognize them due to dementia or Alzheimer's. I am afraid of the indignity that coincides with a long-term illness. The financial consequences of such an illness add to the fear.

3.   I am afraid of dying instantly, without warning, not being able to say goodbye to my loved ones. For example, I think of dying in a plane or car wreck. I have fear of dying quickly of an aneurism or in a nuclear war with thousands of others.

4.   Some people are afraid of losing control. This includes bodily functions, such as a bowel movement, hearing, seeing or thinking clearly. Throughout our life, we devote energy in order to gain control over our future. When we lose control, we feel helpless and hopeless. Because we have little control over when and how we die, fear emerges.

5.   There are those who have a fear of eternal punishment. For me, belief in hell is untenable, if you mean by hell a place you burn eternally after you die. Therefore, I have no fear of eternal punishment. I know of people who report they do not believe there is a hell after they die, nevertheless continue having a degree of fear about the possibility.

6.   Of course, a certain amount of fear is always present when the future is unknown. How a person deals with the unknown throughout their life will probably impact how they deal with the inevitable unknown dimension of death.

7.   Many people fear they will cease existing after death. This fear isn't confined only to the non-religious or atheists. Many people of faith feel insecure about their belief in the afterlife.

8.   I am scared of not being able to die. Throughout my ministry I have been with people who were mad every morning they woke up. Their health had deteriorated to the point where pain, both physical and emotional, was constant and intense. There was no hope it will get any better. As one lady said to me when she could not die and stop the persistent pain, "Why is this taking so long?" There was nothing she could do but wait for death to appear. She felt stuck and afraid.

Most of us have experienced loved ones who lingered in a frail or demented state. I am scared of being one of those persons who wants to die but cannot. I have a fear of being bedridden and debilitated. I am scared of living after my usefulness has passed. All of us prefer a convenient exit where we can go quickly and quietly.

9.   I add the issue of boredom to the fear of being unable to die. I am afraid of being bored. If I were to lose my eyesight, hearing, mobility, or heaven forbid, all three, I would be bored. What would I do with my time if my mind was clear, but my body parts were not functioning?

10. Some fear dying alone. They want to die in their home, surrounded by loved ones, rather than in a hospital.

II. Guilt/Sorry/Remorse/Regrets

Which of the following guilt producing sentences might you say in the face of death? Complete the following sentences. Examining our guilt lessens the degree and frequency of our death anxiety and better prepares us for our end.

- I wish I had never . . .
- If only I had . . .
- If only I had not . . .
- My only regret is . . .
- If I had to do if over again I would have . . .
- I wish I had spent less time . . .
- The next time around I want to spend more time . . .
- I failed to . . .
- I should have given more to . . .
- I wish I had told _____ I love him/her.
- I am disappointed I did not do enough to . . .
- My priorities would have been different and included . . . .
- I wish I had forgiven _____.
- I wish I had accepted forgiveness from _____.
- I never should have . . .

I have always been a pleaser, often to a fault. I feel guilty when I think of the pain my loved ones will experience when they find out I have died. I feel guilty when I think of my death bringing stress and inconvenience to others, especially my family.

My major regret is failing to live the moment to the fullest.

III. Loneliness

Essentially, there are two kinds of loneliness. First, some feel lonely when they are alone. They need to be around people.

A second kind of loneliness is what I refer to as "natural" loneliness. We feel lonely because we exist. It is a natural and inevitable part of being human. Therefore, this kind of loneliness is not something we can eliminate. Getting rid of natural loneliness would be like getting rid of a body part.

Natural loneliness has little to do with whether we are around people. It pertains to being a unique person. There is nobody like us. Therefore, nobody can completely understand what we are feeling and thinking. Hopefully, you have someone who wants to know your inner most thoughts. Nevertheless, ultimately nobody can understand the depth or intensity of our thoughts and feelings, especially about death.

Loneliness is a normal and expected aspect of the death experience. Because dying is inevitable, we naturally feel a degree of helplessness as we contemplate the fragile aspect of life. We feel lonely when we find ourselves helpless.

Life is full of change. Death is definitely a change. Change is accompanied by the unknown. Being insecure about the unknown future imparts loneliness.

At one time in life, all of us have been separated from someone we loved. Remember the loneliness you felt when you left a place or experience you enjoyed? Death is the ultimate separation experience and consequently is accompanied by loneliness.

We find ways to cope with our loneliness, such as throwing ourselves compulsively and anxiously into an endless round of activity. Work, recreation, sex, drugs and sometimes religion are used to escape the feeling of loneliness. Surrounding ourselves with people is a tactic used to cope with loneliness.

In the final analysis each of us travels alone. No matter how close I get to other people, I must still face life alone. This is especially true when it comes to dying. Hopefully, we will have people around us. Nevertheless, the actual act of dying must be done alone, with God by our side.

IV. Mad/Angry

Mad is another feeling I have when it comes to death. I feel angry when I recall all the people who died before their time. I have lived a relatively pain-free life for over 70 years. There are millions of people who died at a very young age from illness and war.

I feel mad at myself when death anxiety, rather than gratitude for life, dominates my thoughts and feelings. Was it luck to be born in the United States and in this time of history? Fortunately, I have had wonderful doctors and multiple opportunities. Nevertheless, the fact remains; I feel mad at myself when my feelings of dying override my gratitude for life.

31

As we prepare for death, it is crucial to deal with the feelings connected to thoughts of death. How can we adequately deal with the feelings whereby we minimize their frequency and intensity? How can we learn to deal with our feelings, so they will not overwhelm and consume us?

We can learn to manage our anxiety in a way that is healthy rather than unhealthy. We can learn to master our emotions rather than allow them to be our slave. We cannot master our fate. We can master the style in which we meet our fate.

I suggest six ways for dealing with the feelings that surround death.

1.   Identify the feelings. When preparing for death, it is crucial to deal honestly with our feelings. Naming and claiming what a person is feeling is one of the first things counselors do to help people deal with their problems/issues. Once a person <u>names</u> and <u>claims</u> his/her feeling, positive things begin to happen.

Trace went to great length describing the situation that brought him to counseling. I asked, "What are you feeling?" He said, "I feel depressed." Knowing the word, depression, can include any number of feelings, I asked Trace to be more specific as to what he was feeling. He used several words, such as anxious, bad and discouraging. These words also circumvented an accurate description of what was at the heart of his feelings. After some time, he was able to identify his lonely and scared feelings. I said to him, "You are halfway towards easing the intensity of your depression. Being able to identify what you are feeling is important as we prepare for death."

Anxiety is the feeling usually associated with death. But the word, anxiety, is too general. Some of the words used to speak of our anxiety are empty, distressed, worried, confused, overwhelmed and futile. These and other feeling words used to describe our death anxiety may be summarized by the three feelings I have mentioned: a. scared/afraid/ fear, b. guilty, regret, c. lonely.

2.   Recognize that sharing a *thought* is different than sharing a *feeling*.

Here are some suggestions on how to distinguish between a thought and a feeling.

Beginning a sentence with "I feel" does not guarantee you have shared a feeling. You have conveyed a thought when you follow "I feel" with the words "like" or "that." For example, a person might say, "I feel anxious when you forget to follow up on our plan." This sentence is expressing a feeling, "anxious." Now insert the word "like" or "that" after the word "feel". It does not make sense and is a hint you are expressing a thought not a feeling. "I feel that/like you will forget to follow up on our plan" expresses a thought, but not the "anxious" feeling.

Here is another hint as to whether you are expressing a thought rather than a feeling. If you can substitute "I am" for "I feel", you have expressed a feeling. For example, *I am* scared when I think of the future. If you can substitute "I think" for "I feel", you have expressed a thought. For example, I feel we should paint the house is expressing a thought rather than a feeling. I am expressing both a thought and a feeling when I say, "When I think about painting the house, I feel overwhelmed."

3.   Accept your feelings as normal. Fear of death is not neurotic. It springs from an accurate perception of reality. We cannot completely get rid of fear, guilt and loneliness.

Philosophers and theologians often use the term "existential" when referring to feelings of loneliness, fear and guilt. Another word for existential is "ordinary". The point is: many feelings arise from simply being a finite human being, as opposed to stemming from some specific life experience. The limitations we have as humans bring forth an expected and normal amount of fear, loneliness and guilt.

At the age of 33, I experienced an event that was extremely helpful as I began traveling down the road of preparing for my death.

I was participating in a therapy group that was part of a continuing education event. I had high admiration for the therapist. One day, he started by asking the question that began every session, "What do you want to work on today?" I had been thinking about this issue for sometime so I immediately spoke up. "I want to work on my fear of dying." I vividly remember his response; "I can help with every fear you have, except the fear of death." I was shocked. Over the course of several weeks I had witnessed how the therapist helped me, as well as some of my colleagues, work through a variety of feelings, including some of our fears. I cannot recall the exact reason he gave for denying my request. I do remember the essence of what he said helped me face reality. His words brought me face to face with the fact that fear of dying is an inevitable and unavoidable part of who we are as human beings. My disappointment turned to relief. A sense of freedom came over me when I accepted the fact that fear of death is a natural and normal part of the human condition. Facing this reality was an important factor in preparing for my death.

4.   Carefully analyze your feelings of fear, loneliness and guilt. I suggest putting a percentage/degree of intensity for each feeling. Examination and analysis reduces the power of a feeling. When I look closely at my feelings, I realize they are not as intense as I thought.

5.   Put your faith and trust in God. Some people profess they have no fear because they trust in God. They quote Bible verses in order to confirm that if faith is strong enough, fear, loneliness and guilt will disappear. If your understanding of God and eternal life takes away your death anxiety, I respect your belief. I believe deeply in God and the power of God for guiding my path and giving me hope for the future. However, when it comes to contemplating my death, faith and trust in God does not completely get rid of my death anxiety.

If faith in God does not eliminate our death anxiety, what good is faith? When I was a little boy there was a cave about a block from our house. My buddies and I would frequently walk to the mouth of the cave, look in, get scared and run back home. One day we ventured into the cave about six steps and retreated again in fear. The darkness of the cave scared us to death. Each time we would go to the cave we challenged ourselves to go a little deeper into the darkness. We never went much farther than five or six steps. We were afraid of what we might meet.

One day I was visiting with an old man who lived next door to us. He would often play catch with me and I would help rake his leaves. I was telling him about our experience at the cave. He said, "Can I go to the cave with you?" "Sure," I said. "But it is scary."

The next morning the old man accompanied me to the cave. As I started into the cave, the man turned on a flashlight. With the light we inched deeper into the cave, farther than I had ever gone. I had not been able to get rid of my fear; but with the light, my fear subsided.

The light of God empowers my life. With it I am able to move forward and deeper into life, even the darkest parts of life. When I trust the light which God provides in Christ, I do not get rid of my feelings; but my death anxiety subsides. Knowing God will be with me in death, as in life, does not eliminate my existential loneliness and fear. It does put it in perspective so my feelings will not paralyze or consume me.

Personally, I have found connecting to God's forgiveness to be a powerful tool for lessening my guilt. To effectively deal with guilt, refer to all the sermons you have heard and all the books you have read on the topic of receiving and giving forgiveness.

6.   Share your feelings with a friend. You may find people are reluctant to talk about death. I trust you will find, at least, one. I have found talking about my feelings associated with death helps lessen the frequency and intensity. Because talking with you about my feelings has helped face my own death, I assume talking about your fears with another person will help you. Reading this book in a discussion group would provide an opportunity to examine and deal with your fears in a healthy way.

I highly recommend including God as one of your friends. God accepts every feeling, without judgment. God even understands the feeling of doubt as to whether God exists. Certainly, God empathizes with our feelings about death.

7.   If these six suggestions do not lessen your death anxiety to your satisfaction, consider visiting with a trained counselor. He/she can assist you in examining your psychological history that may affect the intensity and frequency of your death anxiety more than you realize.

A woman came into my office and had no sooner sat down when she said, "I'm dying." I quickly and glibly responded, "We're all dying." "No," she said. "My doctor just told me I have about six months to live."

I recognize there is a big difference between knowing I am doing to die and receiving the kind of information that came to this woman. I also knew of a helpful way I could respond to her. I could listen to her thoughts and feelings. I could let her unload. I could give reassurance I would be with her along the journey.

We set up another time to talk. I realized I also needed to unload my thoughts and feelings about my own death. Who would want to listen to me with the amount of time and intensity I needed? I have come to the conclusion this book is a response to my need to talk about the thoughts and feelings that fill me as I consider my own death. I hope this book does the same for you.

QUESTIONS FOR CONTEMPLATION
AND DISCUSSION

1. Talk with yourself and/or a friend about which of the 10 fears are most relevant to your life.
2. What guilt and regrets do you have about the past? In what way would naming and claiming those feelings help prepare you for death?
3. How do you respond to the idea that we cannot completely get rid of our fear of death?
4. How do you respond to the idea that ultimately we face death alone?
5. Would it be helpful to share your thoughts and feelings about death with a friend? Why? Why not?

4

Participate in a Miracle

The doorbell rang. I opened the door and there stood my neighbor. He held out to me a beautiful bouquet of flowers and a basket of fruit. "Here," he said. "I want you to have these gifts." I responded, "I deserve your gift. I am a good person. I have done much to earn it. I expected you to give me a gift." I then closed the door.

You probably are thinking, how rude. Nobody would respond to a neighbor's gift in this manner. Was my response ignorant and arrogant? Was I selfish? Did I deserve my neighbor's gift? Did I take for granted that my friend would give me a gift? Most importantly, did I close the door to the opportunity to live as a grateful person?

Life is a gift. The only response that makes sense is gratitude. To think we deserve and earn the gift of life is rude, ignorant and arrogant. Yet, how often do I take the gift of life for granted? How many times have I closed the door to opportunities because I was ungrateful? I am like an immature six-year-old at a birthday party. The child ungratefully opens a gift, focusing on the gift with little thought of being thankful. Yes, nobody would respond this way to a gift, yet how often is this similar to our response to God's gift of life.

Recognizing life is a gift and being grateful are two important ways to prepare for death. When I die, put on my tombstone: "My life was a gift. I just finished participating in a miracle."

Many events in my life have illuminated this truth. One of the most significant happened when I was 72 years old.

Elaine and I were sitting in the back patio of our daughter's house, talking about our plans for playing golf. Kara opened the back door and announced, "My water broke." It was time for my grandchild to be born. We were off to the hospital.

Forty years ago, when our daughter was born, we had a three-minute drive to the hospital. Kara's hospital was about 40 minutes away. We made it in about 25 minutes. In my excitement and sense of urgency, I broke the speed limit and ran several red lights. Kara's husband arrived within the hour and preparation began for the birth.

When our children were born, we did it the old-fashioned way; I sat in the waiting room while my wife was in labor. When our child was born, the doctor came into the room and told me I had a child. In about 30 minutes, I would be able to see my wife and baby. I never witnessed the birth of our children. Now, I found myself in a hospital room with our daughter who was about to give birth to our seventh grandchild. To my surprise, the doctor allowed us to stay in the room and witness the birth.

When the doctor came into the room to deliver the baby, Elaine and I huddled in the corner. I was feeling somewhat guilty being there. I did not know anyone could be in the delivery room except the doctor, nurse and maybe the father. I felt nervous and excited, very excited.

As Kara started to push, I found tears in my eyes. At one point, I dared to venture to the edge of the bed and peer at the vaginal opening where I could see the crown of our grandson's head. In a few minutes, the doctor grabbed the head, pulled the baby into this world and laid him on Kara's chest. The baby and I cried.

Many thoughts went through my head. This identical type of event happened to you and me when we were brought kicking and screaming into this world. As I watched my daughter straining to push out her baby, I had a flashback. I pictured my mother in labor, straining to push me into the world. At one point, I was a fetus in my mother's womb and the next I was a living, breathing human being. I envisioned being laid on my mother's abdomen, crying, shriveled, bloody and ready to live. As I witnessed our grandson's little fingernails, ears, eyes and nose,

I said to myself, "I was just like this, way back when." I thought of my grandchild's tiny kidneys, lungs and heart. Wow, to think I was like that at one time in history. The flashback reminded me again; life is a gift. This awareness has been helpful in preparing for death.

I cannot image myself dead and in a grave. Likewise, I cannot image myself lifeless in my mother's abdomen, initially nothing but an infinitely small seed, invisible to the naked eye.

Babies have a way of reminding us that life is a gift. Notice the expressions on people's faces when they see a newborn child. Rather than thinking about all the problems that lie ahead for the child, the beauty and miracle of life enrapture us.

The gift of life has come to me in the form of good food, hot baths, sunsets, fall leaves, waterfalls, rain, snow and flowers of all sizes and colors. The blessings of a loving family and good friends continually surround me. Even the plains of Kansas and a field of wheat are a beautiful sight. I have taken a float trip down a winding stream and climbed one of the highest mountains in Colorado. I have been humbled by the historical World War II monument at the beaches of Normandy. I have played Monopoly with my kids and grandkids. The pleasure and advantages of various modes of transportation have afforded me the luxury of visiting many wonderful parts of this country and the world. I have ridden on a horse, cruised on a gigantic boat, traveled across the United States on a train and soared through the skies on a jet.

I have savored the taste of oatmeal, mashed potatoes, apples and strawberries. I have enjoyed using the TV remote to view many fascinating programs. I have relished the freedom provided by the gift of living in the United States. The technology of computers and cell phones continue to fascinate me. After my wife was diagnosed with chronic leukemia, I rejoiced when the doctors declared her in remission—the gift of modern medicine.

When I reflect on the gift of life, I often ask myself whether I would prefer to have lived in another era. For approximately 90% of recorded history, securing enough food to eat and fighting wars occupied people's time. There were no flush toilets, switches to flip, washer/dryers, air conditioning, anesthetics or microwave ovens.

I have concluded there is not a time in history better than the present one. For example, I have experienced wonderful benefits of modern medicine. I have had seven surgeries during my lifetime. Without surgery, I would have died at least four times. The other three times, extreme pain would have dominated my being and probably lasted a lifetime. I cannot image what people did in the generations before modern medicine. They died much earlier and lived with pain. Even if you believe being born in this era was luck, it is still a gift.

When children are given a gift, why do parents remind them, "And what do you say?" Do parents teach children to say "thank you" simply because it is the polite thing to do? Parents understand that thankful people ultimately discover more happiness in life, even amidst difficulties.

Recently, I was in a church group who were discussing what happens after we die. I made the comment that my death anxiety is manageable, even though I think about death a lot. One person responded, "That is because of your faith as a Christian." The person concluded my faith in heaven lowered my anxiety.

My faith as a Christian has little to do with the afterlife. For many, faith means having assurance of living in another life with God. This idea of faith is different from my understanding of faith as expressed in the Bible. For me, gratitude is synonymous with faith. Look at the passages in the Bible where Jesus uses the word, faith. Substitute gratitude or thankfulness in the place where the word faith appears. For example, "Go, your faith (gratitude) has made you well." (Mark 5:34) In Matthew 20:21, we read that faith (gratitude) can remove the mountains of life.

Examine the meaning of faith as Paul uses it in Romans and Galatians. Justification by faith is the central theme of Paul's letters. When he speaks of having faith in Jesus Christ, "faith" is a response to God's grace revealed in Jesus. Having faith in Jesus is a grateful response to God's gift of grace. We do not earn or deserve the gift; therefore, gratitude (faith) is the response that makes sense and leads to a fulfilling life. We are justified by thankfulness to God for the gift of grace.

Amidst difficulty and pain and in the presence of death, God's power sustains people who understand faith and gratitude are synonymous.

Recall the scene at the birthday party for a small child. The time comes when the guests surround the birthday boy or girl. The child begins opening the presents. In typical fashion, no sooner is one gift unwrapped before the next gift is grabbed and opened. The process continues until all presents are open, and it does not take much time. The child quickly moves from gift to gift. If he or she pauses to say thank you, it is only for an instant. When the process is completed, a child cannot identify the giver of each gift.

Meanwhile, what are the parents doing? They are writing down the name of the person who gave the gift. Parents know being thankful is an important lesson for children to learn. We may expect a child to forget the giver of a gift, but what about an adult?

Like an immature child, we focus on the gifts of life. We fail to remember the Giver of life and continually express our gratitude.

People who remain thankful amidst the difficulties of life receive life as a gift **and** remember God, the giver of life. The receiving and remembering are translated into power. God's power enables us to remain thankful even in the face of death.

It is easier for someone like me to be grateful for the gift of life than a person who has experienced a life of pain and suffering. I confess that I cannot fully understand what it would be like to live in constant pain, without hope for a better future.

When I was in the fifth grade, a friend gave me a present. I thought it was strange since it was not my birthday. There was no apparent reason for giving me a gift. I asked, "Why are you giving me a gift?" "I just wanted to give you something nice. You are such a good friend, the friend explained." I eagerly unwrapped the box and opened it. Out jumped a slinky figure, hitting me in the face. It scared me. It also hurt, both my feelings and my face. The gift was definitely unexpected and unwanted.

For many, being grateful for the gift of life is like opening a box with a slinky figure. Life is not what they wanted or expected. They have had numerous hurtful experiences, emotionally and physically. Children get cancer and die at an early age. Hundreds die when a tsunami unexpectedly strikes. Millions go to bed hungry every night.

People suffer relentless and unspeakable pain as the result of an incurable, debilitating disease. Wars leave hundreds dead at a very young age.

It is difficult to accept the truth that life is a gift when life is full of inexorable and persistent pain. What if my daughter had died in childbirth or my grandson was born with an incurable disease? Would I glibly declare life is a gift? If I had been a slave on a ship coming to America from Africa, would I be thankful for the gift of life? If my child died at an early age from cancer, would I speak so freely of life being a gift? An answer does not come easily. In the face of these questions, I am hesitant to continue writing about how gratefully receiving life as a gift helps prepare a person for death.

I frequently play golf with my wife. She normally hits the ball straight and in the middle of the fairway. I normally hit the ball left, right or dribble it a few yards ahead. Every once in awhile I hit the ball far and in the middle of the fairway. My wife notices when I am in the middle of the fairway, I am more fun to play with. I talk. I enjoy the game. I am aware of the people around me and the beautiful scenery. When I am playing poorly, the game is anything but enjoyable. I do not appreciate just being able to play.

How can a person gratefully receive life as a gift when their life is out-of-bounds, rather than in the middle of the fairway? I frequently ask this question. The answer comes by looking closely at the lives of those who are qualified to teach us how to be grateful, even when they are not in the middle of the fairway.

I do not feel qualified to talk about how to be thankful amidst the difficulties of life. I was born with a silver spoon in my mouth. My brother is right; I am a golden boy. Yes, I have had the usual problems in my life. However, compared to so many, my life has been a breeze. It is important to remember this book is written by a white, middle-class, American male who is healthy and has received huge amounts of love and attention throughout his life.

Several months ago, I experienced extreme physical pain. The pain lasted for about three days. I said to myself, "Now is the time for the test. Can I be thankful even when it is difficult?" I gave myself a pep talk: "Life is a gift. Be thankful." I wanted to practice what I preach. I was angry at myself. I said, "You big dummy. Throughout your life, 99%

of your time has been pain free. You have so much to be thankful for, and now pain arrives and you falter." I discovered how difficult it was to be thankful when I was in such physical pain. Emotional pain can hurt as much or more than physical pain. I realized if this pain would never let up, I would rather die. I want to learn from the people who are qualified to teach me how to be a grateful person, even when I am experiencing pain.

In my job as a pastor, I have shared with persons at the time of death, pain and suffering. I have found hope from those who have remained thankful, even though their life was difficult. Their witness reassures me that people can continue to be grateful in the midst of evil, suffering and impending death. These people are much more qualified to write this section of the book.

I stand in awe of those who somehow accept whatever life brings to them. I draw comfort from their witness, knowing I can remain a thankful person even amidst my times of pain and suffering.

How do some people accept the difficult parts of life and continue being thankful? Ezra is qualified to answer this question.

Ezra was the tenth of 12 children. At the age of six, his father disappeared. They never heard from him again. All he remembers about his father is that he was either drunk or at work. Ezra's mother assumed responsibility for raising the children. She did fine for a couple of years and then she became hooked on drugs. Ezra began floundering. He started running with kids who were heading into trouble.

Ezra has turned out to be a responsible, well-adjusted and grateful person. Why? He points to his grandmother who believed in him. She encouraged him to fulfill his potential.

People, like Ezra, remain grateful in the midst of difficulties because someone in their life believed in them. I trust you have a person who encouraged you at a time in your life when you could have strayed. It may be a youth sponsor, pastor, friend, family member, teacher or peer. I hope God is on your list of those who gave you power to fulfill your gifts, even when you were discouraged.

Throughout my life and ministry, I have spent a considerable amount of time helping people reconcile their pain and suffering with the truth that life is a gift. People will ask, "Why is this happening?

Why does God allow suffering?" People who remain thankful amidst the difficulties of life resist blaming others, including God. They have a clear and informed understanding of the will of God.

A young couple in our church were expecting their first child. I knew she was due any day. I received a phone call in my office from the mother. "Can you come to the hospital?" she requested. "Our baby was born two hours ago. She is a beautiful eight-pound baby. The doctors have told us she has a rare disease and will live only a few days. I want you to baptize our child."

I rushed to the side of the new parents and baptized the baby. The parents lived at the hospital for the next several days until the baby died. I visited them several times a day. Never once did either the father or mother blame or question God's will.

During the months that followed, I grew close to the parents. We had many serious conversations about life, death, God and the future. When a healthy baby boy was born 14 months after their child died, I decided to ask a question that had been lingering in my mind. "We have shared a lot over the past months. I know your faith in God has been important in helping you make it through the difficult time. When your baby died, how did God fit into that experience? I never heard you ask why would God allow this to happen to your baby." I was not very pleased with how I worded my question, but they seemed fine with giving me an answer. "Neither one of us," said the wife, "gave one thought to the idea that our baby's death was part of God's plan. Why would God will a healthy newborn baby to die? I was taught God is love; and, surely, a loving God would not make such a thing happen. We felt God was with us. We certainly could not have made it without that power."

This young couple remained thankful to God amidst this trying time in their lives. I felt good when they reminded me of a sermon I had preached on the will of God. To understand the will of God, review the many books written and sermons preached on this topic. I shared my ideas on this topic in chapter eight of my book, *Believe the Believable.*

The gift of life includes the freedom to choose. A gift without free choice would not be much of a gift. Suffering and pain are not the will of God, but rather the result of the misuse of our freedom to choose.

Bad and tragic human choices have been extensive and rampant throughout the course of history. The cumulative effect of the destructive decisions that people have made over the years explains most suffering and tragedy. We know the negative consequences of putting into our body certain food and harmful substances. We have yet to grasp the long-term consequences of continual disregard for the environment. These are just two of the ways misuse of our freedom contributes to suffering and contaminates God's gift. We cannot underestimate or fully comprehend the negative and cumulative effects of millions upon millions of humans, over thousands of years, living selfishly. History helps us understand why, for many, life has not turned out to be a wonderful gift

The gift of freedom to choose includes deciding how we are going to respond when life deals us a bad hand. History is full of stories of people who have chosen to make lemonade out of lemons and turn tragedy into triumph. Of course, this is not easy to do. Nevertheless, each person, no matter how difficult life has been, has the freedom to focus on what was gained or dwell on what was lost.

I confess that all too often I use my free will to focus on all the bad things in life. I understand this is not a good use my time. I am not always grateful.

The following analogy has been helpful to me in understanding the will of God.

I have always enjoyed putting together a jigsaw puzzle, especially if it is a large one. The purpose and challenge of the puzzle is, of course, to complete the picture by putting the many pieces together. It can be a frustrating experience because we are unsure where each piece of the puzzle fits. It takes time, patience and a desire to enjoy the process. The finished picture on top of the box serves as an aid in working the puzzle.

The gift of life is like a jigsaw puzzle. It has many pieces/experiences. Death is one of the pieces. The purpose and challenge of life is to put the experiences of life together in a meaningful way. This is often a frustrating experience especially when uncertainly hits us. It takes time, patience and a desire to enjoy the process. Jesus provides a picture of how life is to be lived. Continually referring to this picture is an invaluable

46

aid for remaining thankful when the pieces of life are confusing and we are unsure about some of life's experiences.

Oftentimes, I cannot find a piece that is a key to moving forward and completing the puzzle. I sometimes even question whether the piece exists. In addition, I may have a piece that does not seem to fit anywhere. I have had the experience where I found myself stuck. I had placed a piece where I thought it fit, only to find out I was wrong.

Many times we cannot find a piece of life's puzzle that is a key to moving forward. We thought we had life figured out and then something happens. We have experiences that do not fit our plan for life. We feel stuck. Sometimes we even question whether a desired piece of life even exists.

When a piece of life's puzzle is difficult and does not seem to fit our desires for a full life, viewing the gift of life as a puzzle helps us understand God's will and remain thankful.

When Jack lost an arm in a freak accident, he did not blame God. He blamed himself. His gratitude for life returned when he responded to the truth that God accepts him even amidst sin and failure. God's power sustained Jack through the difficult time. Connecting to God's power of forgiveness and unconditional acceptance enables many to be grateful even when life is not what they want.

Consider this parable as you strive to reconcile the good parts of life with the bad and live thankfully for the gift of life.

The doorbell rings. On the front porch stands a person who hands you an envelope. You open it and gaze upon a set of car keys. The keys are to a brand new car sitting in the driveway. "It is a free gift," says the person who handed you the envelope. Also in the envelope is a gas credit card and papers for a paid-up insurance policy on the car. Both of these items are for the life of the car. Wow, a free car and you did nothing to deserve and earn it.

You enjoy the car for many long years. Oh yes, there were problems. You took it to the repair shop from time to time. You even had a couple wrecks, but the body shop was able to put it back in good shape. As the car got older, there were a few more problems. A remedy was available for each situation.

One day your mechanic says, "Your car is on its last leg. It will not last much longer. You can't expect a car to run forever. You've gotten a lot of good mileage from this car, but it will die soon."

You are not happy. Yes, you knew the car would not last forever, but you are not ready for it to die. In fact, you may be a little angry. This car had taken you many interesting places. Your family and friends had shared this car with you. In this car you have seen beautiful scenery of all kinds, sunsets, lakes, wheat fields, mountains and the changing color of the trees. You definitely are not ready for this car's life to end.

All of a sudden, you realize what a fool you are, an ungrateful fool. You had many years of pleasure with this car. You had free fuel and insurance. Why should you feel anything but total gratitude for having this car as long as you did? It was a gift in the first place. Thankfulness, not regret, is the only response that makes any sense.

I trust you will continually apply the meaning of this parable to your life. The truth will help you remain a thankful person even when life is not working as you would like.

Maitland Sue's lifestyle was one of gratitude. At the age of 56, the doctors informed her that she had a debilitating disease. In a few years, she was unable to walk. She remained thankful for the gift of life. In a few more years, the disease produced pain. Sometimes the pain lasted for an hour and other times for a couple days. When the pain came, Maitland Sue found it difficult to remain thankful. When the pain let up, her thankfulness emerged full and strong. As a small child, her parents taught her the meaning of gratitude. Years of experience as a grateful person enabled her to remain faithful even when it was not easy. The old adage is true: Practice makes perfect.

The best athletes know the importance of practicing. When the game is on the line and the moment is tense, the athletes who emerge successful have been faithful and diligent in practice. When a moment in life is tense and something important is on the line, the people who emerge thankful have been grateful throughout their life. When a difficult event happens, they have the necessary reserves stored up for sustaining them in those tense times.

People die like they live. In other words, a person who has lived life as a thankful person can die a thankful person. These people give me hope that gratitude will sustain me in my hour of death.

People like Maitland Sue are quick to tell us they have their moments. They have hours, days and even weeks when they are discouraged. Nevertheless, because of their grateful lifestyle, they are able to remain thankful to God for the gift of life and the power God constantly gives to them.

On my walk this morning, it finally came to me. Honor is the word I have been looking for. I have always talked of life being a gift. Honor is the word that says how I feel about being alive. It is an honor to receive years of living, feeling, thinking, seeing, hearing, tasting, smelling and experiencing all life has to offer. Gratitude prepares us for death.

I guess this chapter is as good as any to announce what I want at my funeral. My wife, Elaine, reminds me that preparing for death includes writing your own funeral plans. This word is for the preacher: Keep it short, no more than four or five minutes. Simply quote the hymn, "O love That Will Not Let Me Go." Throughout my life, this has been my theme song. It expresses my faith in life and in death.

"O love that wilt not let me go, I rest my weary soul in Thee. I give Thee back the life I owe . . ."

Tell the folks I tried to approach each day as a gift from God. It is a gift I did not earn or deserve. The only response that makes sense, or at least makes sense to me, is gratitude. I lived and I died eternally grateful to God for the gift of life. I got much more from life than any one person deserves. See, this did not take even five minutes. A short funeral is good.

QUESTIONS FOR CONTEMPLATION
AND DISCUSSION

1. Is it difficult to affirm life is a gift? Why? Why not?
2. What life experiences have been so painful that you were unable to remain thankful?
3. Who has been an inspiration to you when it comes to remaining thankful amidst the difficult times of life?
4. How do you understand God's will in the face of pain and suffering?
5. How does the parable of the new car apply to your life?

5

WHEN DEATH
BECOMES A GIFT

L ife is a gift. Death, as part of life, is therefore also a gift. For me, an important and helpful way to prepare for dying is to view death as a gift.

I recall leading a study group at the church. In the discussion, I mentioned my belief that death is a gift. My comment disturbed one woman. Her husband had recently died. Experiencing the death of her loved one did not feel like a gift. Her husband's death was unexpected and painful. Yes, she was drawing strength from her husband's gifts, gifts that live on within her spirit. Nevertheless, she was struggling to view death as a gift.

It was mid-February and the ground was covered with two inches of snow. I received word that my good friend had a heart attack. About five years ago, he had bypass surgery. I phoned him. "I have a tee time this afternoon at two o'clock. I expect you to be there. I don't want to hear any lame excuses, such as the weather or your health. I want to play golf." I was relieved when he responded to my light-hearted approach by saying, "I'll be there, but I might not be in my usual championship form. Even though my health isn't the best, I can still beat your butt."

As we talked on the phone, he was waiting to hear from the doctors as to the results of the attack and the prognosis. He knew I was writing a book on death and said, "I'm interested in what you are writing about death. As you can imagine, I have been thinking about death a lot more lately." I told him I would welcome some feedback. "Would you be willing for me to send you a chapter and give me your response?"

After reading what I had written, he emailed his reaction. "Waiting to hear the test results is killing me and I'm anxious about my future. You say that death is a gift. Maybe you mean to say that 'mortality' is a gift. We are all mortal. Right now, I am finding it hard to see death as a gift."

As I write this chapter, I acknowledge, when a person is experiencing pain and/or when his/her own death may be imminent, seeing death as a gift can be very difficult. My friend's comment pointed out that when I say death is a gift, I mean awareness of our mortality can be a gift.

Six positive experiences happen in life when we choose to live with the understanding that our mortality can be a gift.

I.   Death becomes a gift when the awareness stimulates us to live each moment to the fullest.

Most of us have been asked, "What if you have only a year or six months to live?" The question implies we would live differently. The most common answers include traveling and spending additional time with the family. We would make each day count. We would scale down the amount of time spent squandering our days and moments. We would cherish each moment. Embracing each day and hour would become part of our lifestyle.

If you had only one year to live, how would you live it? Each person will answer this question differently. The answer depends upon multiple factors such as personality characteristics, life experiences, genetic makeup, psychological history and age.

In my earlier years, why did I spend so much time squandering precious moments? When I was younger, my thoughts were predominately about the past or the future. Death felt like an event in the distant future. Cherishing the moment was not something I did, at least not very frequently. I confess being in my early 40's before beginning each day with the vow, "I am grateful for one more day." In recent years, these words are my affirmation of faith and part of my daily ritual. I only wish this affirmation and ritual had been present throughout my life. Why did I wait until . . . ?

Now, in the autumn of my life and with fewer moments to live, I am more motivated to treasure each moment. Embracing each moment feels more urgent at the age of 73 than it did at 23. I am writing this chapter hoping you will be motivated to take pleasure in each moment and resist waiting until you are older.

What if you had only one day to live? A more revealing and provocative question is, what if you died and could come back for a day? Would you want to do this? And what day and age would you choose? In dramatic fashion, Thorton Wilder addresses the question of how we would live if we had only a day to live.

In the final act of Wilder's play, *Our Town*, Emily, who died giving birth to her second child, has been given the chance to go back home to a time she has chosen. She picks her 12th birthday. Emily thinks she can return to the world of the living and revisit and re-experience the past. With the help of the Stage Manager and against the advice of those who also have died, Emily returns to the living. "I can't bear it. They're so young and beautiful. Why did they ever have to get old? Mama, I'm here. I'm grown up. I love you all, everything. I can't look at everything hard enough. Oh, Mama, just look at me one minute as though you really saw me. Mama, 14 years have gone by. I'm dead. You're a grandmother, Mama. I married George Gibbs, Mama. Wally's dead, too. Mama, his appendix burst on a camping trip to North Conway. We felt just terrible about it—don't you remember? But, just for a moment now we're all together. Mama, just for a moment we're happy. Let's look at one another. I can't. I can't go on. It goes so fast. We don't have time to look at one another. I didn't realize all that was going on in life and we never noticed. Take me back—up the hill—to my grave. But first: Wait! One more look. Good-bye, Good-bye, world. Good-bye, Grover's Corners? Mama and Papa. Good-bye to clocks ticking and Mama's sunflowers. And food and coffee. And new-ironed dresses and hot baths and sleeping and waking up. Oh, earth, you're too wonderful for anybody to realize you. Do any human beings ever realize life while they live it, every minute? I'm ready to go back. I should have listened to you. That's all human beings are! Just blind people."

Emily's words inspire me. I want to notice everything going on in life. It all goes so fast. One more look. I want to realize life while I have it.

Appreciating each moment comes through fully activating the five sense organs: seeing, hearing, smelling, touching and tasting.

I began wearing contact lenses when I was about 30 years old. It was in the day of hard lenses. Because of a harsh reaction to the hard lenses, I developed a painful eye abrasion. The only way to deal with the pain was to keep my eyes closed for about a 24-hour period. During the time when I could not see, I vowed never again to take for granted the gift of sight. I promised myself I would make certain to see, really see. I am disgusted with myself when I recognize how often I have failed to keep my promise and see all the beauty around me.

I recall a summer vacation when I developed a pain in my stomach. The pain continued for over 24 hours. I cut the vacation short and checked into the local hospital. I vividly remember the doctor coming into my room and informing me that I had hepatitis. Several months prior, I had a friend who died from hepatitis. Needless to say, I was scared to death. This was before the doctor informed me there were several kinds of hepatitis. I would get well within a week or so.

I was quarantined for several hours. Only my wife could visit me. I yearned to be with our two boys who were seven and five at the time. To satisfy my need and pass the time, Elaine brought the boys to the yard outside my hospital window. They waved at me and played touch football together. When I returned home, I hugged my boys like never before. Just touching them reminded me how important touch is to my happiness.

The doctor told me there were certain foods I should refrain from eating until the hepatitis passed from my body. One of those was cantaloupe. You guessed it; I craved cantaloupe. We will savor food when we cannot have food or certain kinds of food. Many times throughout my life I have been so sick I could not eat. During this time, I vowed never again to take eating for granted. I will savor each bite. I have failed to keep my promise. All too often, rather than really enjoying the gift of taste, my mind has been on other things that could have waited until I savored my food.

I have never lost my hearing. However, a wonderful man in our church unexpectedly developed an illness that resulted in loss of hearing. He was an outgoing guy who loved music. When I visited him, I had to write on a notepad what I wanted to say. Every time I left his house, I renewed my gratitude for being able to hear. Even today, years later, I think of my friend and embrace the opportunity to hear.

Do we have to witness someone who cannot walk before we treasure the simple act of walking? What if you could not smell the fragrance of a flower? Death becomes a gift when it motivates us to cherish the moment by taking pleasure in the five senses.

Several years ago, I had a problem with my prostate. I had to wear a catheter for one week. It was extremely uncomfortable. I promised myself I would never again take for granted the gift of relieving myself. I am disgusted with myself when I think of how often I have failed to keep my promise and take this simple bodily function for granted. The traditional five senses do not include peeing. Nevertheless, during that week, peeing became as important as seeing and hearing.

Through procrastination and preoccupation, we fail to live the moment to the fullest. American psychologist, Abraham Maslow, says, "The ability to be in the present moment is a major component of mental wellness."

In the book, *New Passages,* Gail Sheehy writes: "We need to change the way we measure time and to relax our insistence on control . . . Instead of focusing on the time running out, it should be a daily exercise in the third age to mark the moment . . . Each moment is like a snowflake, unique, unspoiled, unrepeatable, and can be appreciated in its surprisingness . . . You want to live in the moment as much as you possibly can . . . If every day is an awakening, you will never grow old. You will just keep growing."

Eckhart Tolle's book, *The Power of Now,* was published in 1998 and made the New York Times bestseller list in 2002. He writes, "The quality of your consciousness at this moment is what shapes the future—which, of course, can only be experienced as the Now."

In his poem, *Eternity*, William Blake writes about living each moment.

> *He who binds to himself a joy*
> *Does the winged life destroy;*
> *But he who kisses the joy as it flies*
> *Lives in eternity's sunrise.*

As I reflect on the time with our children, I wanted to kiss the joy as it flies. I embraced those moments when Kara and I took a ride on the cycle. I kissed the joy as I taught tennis to Kip and played basketball with Kevin.

Yesterday, my wife asked me to join her on the back porch swing. I quickly dropped what I was doing and responded to her request.

I want the gift of death to motivate me to kiss each moment as it flies. I destroy the moment if I try to grab it, rather than fully embracing each experience of life and moving on.

Athletes and sport psychologists speak of "staying in the moment". This approach maximizes an athlete's potential. An athlete knows his/her ability is impaired by focusing on what has happened in the past and/or might take place in the future. Our ability to live life to the fullest is impaired by focusing on the past and future. We maximize our potential by choosing to stay in the moment.

Athletes who perform to their potential understand what they can and cannot control. They cannot control what has happened in the past or may happen in the future. If athletes allow themselves to let past mistakes and decisions occupy their thoughts, the outcome will be negatively affected. They can control what is happening in the moment. Fulfilling our potential in life comes by retaining control over what we can control, such as living the present moment to the fullest.

Professional athletes develop techniques for focusing on what is happening in the moment. The techniques reduce negative thoughts. The techniques are usually in the form of a ritual. For example, a tennis player, each time before serving, may bounce the ball a certain amount of times. As a method of dealing with the pressure before shooting a free throw, a basketball player will repeat a specific motion. These rituals/

techniques keep an athlete's mind on what is happening at the time, rather than becoming distracted by something that happened in the past or might take place in the future.

For the athlete, the techniques are more than a matter of concentration. The techniques we may develop for staying in the moment will be more than concentration. Because the brain has a small capacity for concentration, attaining a state of mind where we are aware all day long is a waste of time and energy.

Numerous psychological and religious books and articles offer suggestions/ techniques on how to limit worry about the past and future. I "Googled" the words, "staying in the moment", and thousands of sites appeared. One site was entitled, "100 ways to live in the moment". Some of the suggestions were helpful, although difficult to apply. Others are too simplistic for what I consider to be a challenging task.

If you are familiar with addiction recovery, you know living life one day at a time is a major part of a successful recovery. A major part of recovering meaning in life is living one day at a time.

No one lives entirely in the present. We cannot eliminate thoughts of the past and future. We remember and we expect. We are subject to traditions and attracted by promises of the future. What we do each day becomes part of an unalterable past and determines what is still possible.

Some thoughts about the past and future are necessary and desirable. I have found thinking about certain past events can be helpful in living the moment to the fullest. I have also discovered some thoughts about the future add pleasure to the present moment. The challenge is to incorporate thoughts of the past and future into the present moment in a way that is healthy rather than harmful.

Thinking about the past can keep us from being in the present. Feelings related to the past, such as guilt, resentment, sadness and worry, keep a person from embracing the moment. Refusing to forgive and/or receive forgiveness will keep a person from enjoying life.

Nevertheless, the past holds potential for enabling us to cherish the moment. We can learn from the past. The poet and philosopher George Santayana said, "Those who cannot remember the past are condemned to repeat it." Some aspects of the past can enrich our thoughts and enhance the present.

Playing the movies of my mind helps ensure that thoughts of the past enhance the present. I select a pleasant past event/experience. In my mind, I play the event like a movie. I can decide how long I want to watch it. If there is an unpleasant part of the movie, I simply fast forward. I select scenes from the movie that contribute good thoughts to my present moment. Good memories can be a source of power for treasuring the moment.

One movie I play frequently is my basketball career. I was a starter in every basketball game I played except one. I was a junior in college and we were playing the number one team in the nation. The coach did not start me that one game. In fact, I did not play the entire game. It is a painful memory. When I allow myself to play that part of the movie, I fail to live the present to the fullest. Therefore, I simply decide to watch the sections of my basketball career movie when I played excellently. I delete and/or fast forward the painful parts of the past. This enhances my days, hours and minutes. I even hit the pause button when I come to the part of the movie where I looked good.

Another way of playing the good movies of my mind is to recall times in the past for which I am grateful. I recall the old song, "When I'm weary and I can't sleep, I count my blessings instead of sheep and I fall asleep counting my blessings."

I confess my thoughts about the future keep me from taking pleasure in each moment. Too often, those thoughts include anxiety about what will or might happen in the future.

Thoughts of the future need not deter us from living the present. Thoughts about the future can help us live each moment. The problem is when our thoughts of the future are full of anxiety and fear. In many incidences, planning for the future is important and necessary. For example, planning and preparing for death helps turn the event into what I want.

The words of John Greenleaf Whittier have helped my thoughts of the future contribute positively to the present.

I know not what the future hath
    of marvel or surprise,
Assured alone that life and death
    God's mercy underlies.
I know not where those islands lift
    their fronded palms in air;
I only know I cannot drift
    beyond God's love and care.

Knowing God's power is available in the future, no matter what the future might bring, helps ensure thoughts about the future will not distract me from living the moment to the fullest.

My experience in the dentist office reminded me how thoughts of the past and future can help us embrace the moment, even when filled with pain.

As I was in the process of writing this chapter, I spent four sessions in the dentist office getting a root canal. Each session brought more pain. This included my back aching from the 50 minutes in the chair with my mouth wide open and my jaw being pulled back to the max. As I was experiencing the trauma, I said to myself, "Being mentally tough, staying in the moment and living each moment to the fullest is not easy when I am in the midst of pain."

As I was experiencing the pain, I began to think of pleasant things in the past. I let my mind go to the future and what I wanted to do for fun after the ordeal was finished. Thinking about the past and future seemed to be better than living the present moment to the fullest. In fact, I found my thoughts about the past and future actually helped me to live this pain-filled moment, even though I would have preferred a different event. My point is this: times of pain make it extremely difficult to enjoy the moment to the fullest. The experience in the dentist office helped me realize that I possess the power of choosing to let thoughts of the past and future work for me and not against me.

I recognize there are degrees of pain. For example, the pain in the dentist chair was not as severe as experiencing the death of a loved one. There are times in life when living the moment to the fullest will be postponed due to unbearable pain.

But, what about pain? How can a person treasure, enjoy and cherish each moment when the moment is filled with pain, emotional and/or physical? This is not an easy thing to do, <u>and</u> it can be accomplished.

In his book, *Ageless Body, Timeless Mind*, Deepak Chopra addresses the important issue of how we can live the moment to the fullest even when we are experiencing pain. Chopra writes, "To feel an emotion fully and completely, to experience it and then release it, is to be in the present, the only moment that never ages . . . Buried hurt disguises itself as anger, anxiety, guilt, and depression. The only way to deal with these layers of pain is to find out what hurts as the pain occurs, deal with it and move on. Living the present means being honest enough to avoid the easy emotion, which is anger, and expose the hurt, which is harder to confront. When hurt is not resolved in the present, the vicious buildup of anger, anxiety, guilt and depression can only grow worse . . . Coming to the moment by putting your attention on the pain allows you to release the pain as soon as it occurs. This release occurs naturally—it is what the body wants to do—and attention is the healing power that triggers it; you observe the pain without getting wrapped up in all the secondary blame, avoidance and denial that usually follows . . . As you learn to say, "I feel hurt," and really be with that feeling, more openness will develop. The emotions that frighten us are the complex ones, because they overwhelm the natural release mechanism. You cannot simply release guilt or depression. They are secondary formations that arose once you forgot how to release hurt. The more hurt you honestly feel, the more comfortable you will be with pain, because the ability to release it will grow . . . No one can really hurt you unless you give them the power to do so. This power lies in your own unresolved pain . . . Live in the present. It is the only moment you have. Keep your attention on what is here and now; look for the fullness in every moment. Accept what comes to you totally and completely so that you can appreciate it, learn from it, and then let it go."

Cherishing each moment to the fullest is a continual challenge for me. For example, last night I took my last shower and ate my last meal; at least this is what I told myself. Rather than worrying about something that happened in the past or might happen in the future,

I made certain to feel the soothing rush of the warm water and savor each bite of food.

Throughout history, people have reacted to the possibility that the world may end some day. Some have even predicted the day. We can be anxious about the future and we can worry about the past. It makes more sense to live the present moment to the fullest and kiss the joy as it flies.

Each morning, I begin my day with a prayer that the awareness of death will motivate me to enjoy each moment of the day to the fullest. I pray that any thoughts I may have about the past and future will enhance my moments.

Treasuring each moment to the fullest is not an easy thing to do. I confess that I am more proficient at embracing each moment when I have good health and sufficient financial resources for food, shelter and health insurance.

Like any skill, there is a learning curve. This includes accepting the fact that no one can continually stay in the moment. Nevertheless, we can become more proficient through patience and practice.

How can a person live each moment to fullest when they are thinking about death? While I was doing my exercises this morning, I asked myself this question. I was pleased with my answer. I have been working on this book for several years, thinking a lot about my own death. I discovered, to my pleasure and surprise, thinking about death has not lessened my enjoying each moment. In fact, it has done the opposite. Thoughts of dying elevate my desire to embrace each moment. I wish the same for you.

II. The second way awareness of our own death becomes a gift is when it motivates us to cherish relationships.

Throughout my ministry, it has been my honor to spend a considerable amount of time with those whose loved ones have died. Repeatedly, I have heard people say, "I wish I had said or done things differently. If only I had apologized to them. I wish I had told them how much I loved them. I should not have been so preoccupied and spent more time with him/her. The resentment I held over the years was so unnecessary." Death reminds us how we can wait too long before we forgive and receive forgiveness.

At funerals, I have witnessed family members resolving past hurts. Reconciliation replaced separation. Conversations ensued about issues previously buried in feelings of resentment. Death inspired people to do and say loving things that had been long overdue. Death is a gift because it keeps before me how important a person is in my life, how his/her gift of love provides energy for my spirit.

Elaine and I have been married 50 years. We often ask ourselves why we have a good marriage. There are several answers. We share them in our book, *KISS AND TELL.*

Our marriage book failed to include one answer: the reality of death has strengthened our marriage. Like every couple, we have our arguments. As we have grown older and are closer to death, we find our arguments are fewer. We credit this to letting ourselves be aware of our mortality. When a topic arises that in the past has produced tension and even a fight, death's reality has a way of keeping the disagreement from escalating. When I think about not having Elaine around me, things that used to bother me quickly become inconsequential. I find myself saying, "Why would I get so worked up over what she just said? Is it really important?" In this way, thinking about death is a gift to our married love.

III. Awareness of our death becomes a gift when it keeps our priorities clear.

After my father's death my mother said, "I have only one regret. I spent too much time doing housework rather than enjoying a summer evening, sitting with your father on the front porch."

I was 24 years old when my father died at the age of 59. Prior to that time, I consumed myself with growing up, playing basketball, college, seminary and marriage. I regret that I did not communicate how I felt about him. I wish I had asked him certain questions.

I did not make the same mistake with my mother who died ten years later. I intentionally had lunch with her about once a month. I asked all my questions and made sure I told her about my love for her and all she did for me. This included teaching me to play Ping Pong when I was in grade school and reading me the Sunday comics. The gift of death precipitated these feelings and events.

Think of the time you got upset about something. In the face of death, it is much easier to see how inconsequential it really was. Death reminds me what is important and, therefore, a gift. Death helps us live the truth, to not sweat the small stuff. Death enables me to recognize how ridiculous it is to get upset about many things. I want to keep my energy focused on things that really matter.

I have considered having my funeral before I die. The second reason is because I want to hear the nice things people will say about me. The first reason is because funerals are times when people wake up to what is important to life. Funerals are often accompanied by new and renewed commitments to the truths and priorities of God. As with my life, I want my death to move people to a deeper commitment to God and God's purposes. So go ahead and have my funeral while I am alive. I want to rejoice in the renewed commitments people make.

Death reminds us that the most satisfying, dependable and refreshing experiences of life lie in the simple things. Death strikes a chord reminding me to find true and lasting happiness in simple gifts. The contemplation of death has changed many of my values, such as re-defining what it means to be successful.

"Simple Gifts" was written by Elder Joseph while he was at the Shaker community in Alfred, Maine, in 1848. These are the lyrics to his one-verse song:

Tis the gift to be simple, 'tis the gift to be free,
'Tis the gift to come down where we ought to be,
And when we find ourselves in the place just right,
Twill be in the valley of love and delight.
When true simplicity is gain'd,
To turn, turn will be our delight,
Till by turning, turning we come round right.

Two additional, non-Shaker verses have been written for the song:

Tis the gift to be loved and that love to return,
Tis the gift to be taught and a richer gift to learn,
And when we expect of others what we try to live each day,
Then we'll all live together and we'll all learn to say,
(refrain)
Tis the gift to have friends and a true friend to be,
Tis the gift to think of others not to only think of "me",
And when we hear what others really think and really feel,
Then we'll all live together with a love that is real.

Several recording artists have sung the following words, expressing how the gift of death can keep us focused on what is important.

The moon belongs to everyone,
The best things in life are free.
The stars belong to everyone,
They gleam there for you and me.
The flowers in spring, the robins that sing,
The moonbeams that shine, they're yours, they're mine.
And love can come to everyone,
The best things in life are free.

IV. Death becomes a gift when it reminds us that without death, life would be even more chaotic.

Imagine what life would be like if there were no death, only birth. More importantly, imagine what this world would be like if the life span was closer to 200 years old rather than 100. Greed, selfishness and irresponsibility would be rampant, even more than the world is currently encountering. Chaos would reign.

V. Death becomes a gift when it levels the playing field.

Alexander the Great, seeing Diogenes looking attentively at a parcel of human bones, asked the philosopher what he was looking for. Diogenes' replied: "That which I cannot find, the difference between your father's bones and those of his slaves."

Peter Kreeft tells us that in the Latin rite for the burial of an Austrian emperor, the people carry the corpse to the door of the great monastic church. They strike the door and say, "Open." The abbot inside says, "Who is there?" "Emperor Karl, the king of . . ." The response from inside: "We know of no such person here." So the people strike the door again. "Who is there?" asks the abbot. "Emperor Karl." "We know of no such person here." So they strike a third time. "Who is there?" asks the abbot again. "Karl," say the people. And the door is opened.

Around the 8th century BC, the Greek poet, Homer, wrote in *Iliad*, "And they die an equal death—the idler and the man of mighty deeds." Jesus proclaimed this truth, "The first shall be last, and the last first." (Matthew 19:30)

The practice of comparing oneself with another is the source of much unhappiness. Some people feel inferior and inadequate because of the advantages they perceive come to others who have money and physical beauty. Conversely, others feel superior because of the favors they enjoy due to their wealth and talent.

Death puts in proper perspective the tendency to afford greater importance to those who have more. How useless are money and appearance in the face of death. To any who continue to live as if money and physical appearance have signficant value, let the words of Jesus ring loud and clear, "You fool! This very night your life is being demanded of you; and the things you have prepared, whose will they be?" (Luke 12:20) "For we brought nothing into the world, so that we can take nothing out of it . . . Those who want to be rich fall into tempation and are trapped by many senseless and harmful desires that plunge people into ruin and destruction." (I Timothy 6:7)

When we acknowledge every human being bleeds the same color and everyone dies, the world of appearances becomes inconsequential. Death is a powerful force that erases the differences among people. The highest and mightiest are brought low by death. Death is definitely a gift and makes the world a better place.

The leveling effect of death is clarified as we proclaim and hear the Gospel truth of grace, God's unconditonal love.

VI. Awareness of our own death becomes a gift when it directs us to the things of God.

My thoughts of death are powerful motivators for making life what God intended and what I want my life to become. The gift moves me to ask the ultimate questions of life, such as what is the meaning of life and how can I make my life count. In the face of death, I look for more God moments in my life.

Mortality prompts me to take responsibility for making this a better world. In the face of death, I want my life to count. I am extremely selfish and self-centered. I do not want to be disturbed or troubled. Death challenges me to focus on giving back even if it means being disturbed or troubled. Death challenges me to smell the roses and also to share the roses with others. This gift of death reminds me that ultimately life is measured by donation not duration. I know down deep Jesus was right when he said, "Those who lose their life will find it."

Death is a gift because it leads me to live and love in such a way that through my witness, my grandchildren will learn that making this a better world is the only way to live.

The story is told of a scene in a courtroom in the early days of our nation. There was a terrible storm. Lightning and thunder filled the air. All of a sudden, the lights flashed off. The room became completely dark. Someone stood up and yelled, "The end of the world is coming. My preacher told me it would happen soon." The judge pounded his gavel and said, "Quiet. It may be the end of the world; but if it is let us, at least, be found faithful in doing our duty. Bring in the candles."

The future is unknown. The end may or may not be near. Meanwhile, bring in the light of Christ. This light enables us to be faithful in doing our duty of living God's truth.

QUESTIONS FOR CONTEMPLATION
AND DISCUSSION

1. In what ways would your life be different if you decided to live each moment to the fullest?
2. What about the past and future keeps you from living the moment to the fullest?
3. How can you use thoughts of the past and future to enhance the present moment?
4. Make a list of the ten most important things/events/people in your life, in order of priority. How might death awareness alter your priorities? Is a specific way of giving back on your list?
5. Do you agree with the author's perspective that chaos in our world would increase if life expectancy were closer to 200 years?

6

WHAT HAPPENS AFTER WE DIE?

Throughout my ministry as a pastor, people frequently asked what I believe happens after we die. I guess they think, because I am a pastor, I should have the answer. My honest response is, I do not know. While this answer seems obvious to me, many respond with disappointment and surprise. After all, an ordained person should know about heaven and eternal life. Most of those, who ask the question, hope their pastor will reassure them that when they die life will not end.

I understand the unenthusiastic response to my answer. Belief in an afterlife is central to most people's belief in God. Recently, I conducted an informal and limited survey in several church study groups. I asked the participants how important belief in heaven is to their Christian faith. Nine out of 10 indicated heaven is very important to their belief.

Since the dawn of history, many have believed humans do not simply cease to exist upon their death. Numerous religions and cultures teach that the physical body may die and decompose; however, something more is in store for us in an "afterlife."

Between 1972 and 1982, when the Roper Center for Public Opinion Research asked the American public, "Do you believe there is life after death," 70 percent responded yes. In 1996, when the Roper Center asked the same question, 73 percent of respondents said yes. A

2002 poll, conducted by the National Opinion Research Center at the University of Chicago, revealed similar results. Seventy-two percent of those polled said they believed there is life after death, 17 percent did not and 11 percent were undecided. In the more recent surveys, the proportion of the U.S. population believing in an afterlife remains constant. Depending on which survey you examine and on any number of variables, belief in heaven and an afterlife ranges between 70% and 85%. The percentage is higher for those who are regular churchgoers.

I find it helpful and informative to look at the various reasons why people believe there is more after we die.

1. Some people's belief in the afterlife is shaped by their fear of dying. It is comforting to know there is more after death. The thought of living forever in heaven helps people deal with their fear, loneliness and guilt. Belief in the afterlife provides a degree of control over what we ultimately cannot control.

2. Many believe in heaven because that is what they were taught.

The preacher was getting irritated. Every Sunday, about five minutes into his sermon, a man on the fourth row would fall asleep. One Sunday he decided to do something about it. In a low tone, he said to the congregation, "Everyone who wants to go to heaven please stand up." Everyone stood up except the man who continued to sleep. After asking the people to be seated, the preacher said, "Everyone who wants to go to hell, please," and then he yelled into the microphone, "Stand up." The man was startled from his slumber and immediately stood up. Looking around and seeing everyone seated he said, "Pastor, I don't know what we're voting on, but it looks like you and me are the only ones for it."

I was taught to believe if you are good, you go to heaven; and if you are bad, you go to H. E. double toothpicks. As a kid, we would not even say the word because we were afraid of going to hell for swearing. This understanding of heaven and hell did not make sense to me; but it seemed as if everyone believed it, so guess I should also.

3. Heaven, as a reward for good behavior, is a common belief. Many think having a reward in heaven is essential if people are to act morally. Without assurance of a reward in the afterlife, people would be irresponsible. There would be even more evil in the world. We need heaven to keep people in line, so goes the argument.

According to a NEWSWEEK poll, 75 percent of Americans believe their actions on earth determine whether they will go to heaven. Many believe living a good life entitles them to live in heaven.

Christianity is not the only religion that has this belief. People of other religions also share it. Groups like Hamas and Islamic Jihad preach the reward message to would-be suicide bombers. Heaven promises martyrs easy access to God, better conditions in the hereafter. As recently as the 1980s, during the Iran-Iraq war, thousands of Iranian soldiers died while walking headlong into Iraqi artillery and land mines, certain of their reward in the hereafter. Moderate Muslim scholars dispute this fundamentalist belief.

The reward philosophy is a central part of religion and also our culture. We have come to believe we are entitled to a reward if we live a good life. You will be rewarded if you work hard and keep your nose clean. "Anyone can make it in our society if they work hard" is a common belief. The question I continually ask is whether we need a cosmic carrot dangled in front of us before we can determine and do what is right and wrong.

Punishment and/or the threat of it motivate children to be good.

What about heaven as a reward for good behavior? Good behavior that arises from the lure of a reward, on the surface, seems like a positive thing. However, this reward theology lacks the necessary power in order for good behavior to endure amidst difficult times. I used punishment to get my children to behave. I also realize my unconditional love was and is more powerful and durable.

Why be good if there is no reward? Many contend that without our points-and-rewards system we will lose our moral compass. I believe it is important to examine our incentive for being a good person. Good behavior, as a response of gratitude for unconditional love rather than a concern for personal reward, holds out more hope for a better world and emotional healthy individuals. Being a good person because we are grateful carries more promise and power than concern for a reward.

There have to be consequences for bad behavior; e.g. if you break the speed limit or shoot someone with a gun, there should be consequences. I also know that gratitude, not the system of rewards and punishments, will ultimately prevail as the only sure foundation and motivation for moral behavior.

In his book, *Unconditional Love*, John Powell writes: "The tension between self-fulfillment directly sought and self-fulfillment as a by-product of loving is, in my judgment, the greatest crisis facing our society today." (p.60)

4. I have experienced pain in my life, physical and emotional. However, my pain has always been temporary. I have little understanding of living with pain that lingers. I can understand why people whose pain continues day after day, would long for something more and better when they die. For these people, I am sure there is relief knowing death will end these experiences and something better awaits them.

For example, the slaves who came over on boats from Africa certainly longed for a better life after they died. I have chosen to share the following description of the slave ship conditions. I believe this history is important to the health and welfare of our nation and the world. Many of the old Negro spirituals speak to the hope for a better life in the next world.

"Grated hatchways between decks enclosed the slaves. The space was so low that they sat between each other's legs. They were stowed so close together there was no possibility of their lying down or changing their position, by night or day. Because they belonged to different individuals, the owners branded them like sheep. These were impressed under their breasts or on their arms, burnt with the red-hot iron. Over the hatchway stood a ferocious-looking fellow with a scourge of many twisted thongs in his hand, who was the slave driver of the ship, and whenever he heard the slightest noise below, he shook it over them and seemed eager to exercise it. How was it possible for such a number of human beings to exist, wedged together and shut out from light or air. This happened while the thermometer, exposed to the open sky deck, was 90 degrees.

The space between decks was divided into two compartments three feet three inches high; the size of one was 16 feet by 18 and of the other 40 by 21. Into the first were crammed the women and girls, into the second the men and boys. 226 fellow creatures were thus thrust into one space 288 feet square and 336 into another space 800 feet square, giving to the whole an average of 23 inches and to each of the women not more than 13 inches. The heat of these horrid places was so great and the odor so offensive that it was quite impossible to enter them, even had there been room. Many destroyed one another in the hopes of procuring room to breathe; men strangled those next them, and women drove nails into each other's brains. Suicide attempts occurred daily and in painfully cruel ways. Slaves tried jumping overboard and even asked others to strangle them. One of the most common ways to avoid further punishment on the journey was to avoid eating. Starvation and suicide attempts became so common that a device was introduced to force slaves, who refused to eat, to open their mouths. Slaves believed their death would return them to their homeland and to their friends and relatives. To prevent slaves from killing themselves, sailors began chopping the heads off corpses implying when they died, they would return to their homes headless."

If I had been one of those slaves, I would have had a need to believe in a better afterlife.

There are many stories of people who have spent their entire life in pain, physical and/or emotional. Without hope of heaven, some would succumb to a deep-seated psychosis, robbing life of any meaning and purpose.

It has been estimated that the twentieth century was the bloodiest in human history. Over a hundred million people were killed and wounded. These facts motivate many to believe in an afterlife.

5. Some people's motivation for believing in heaven stems from the stories of near death experiences (NDE). Modern technology has been effective in resuscitating people who, to all intents and purposes, were clinically dead. People, who have been at the point of death and survived, tell stories of how they experienced the "other side". They

talk of some form and degree of a continuation of consciousness. For some this is evidence and proves there is more after we die.

According to a 1992 Gallup poll, approximately five percent of Americans have experienced a near-death experience, about 15 million adults. Over the last 30 years, deathbed visions and end-of-life experiences have been the topic of numerous books and articles. You can read individual stories of near death experiences in such books as *The Art of Dying,* by Peter and Elizabeth Fenwick. It is interesting to read many of the perspectives on this topic.

I Googled "Top Ten Books of near death experiences." There are numerous theories on the origin of NDE. Are near death experiences imagination or wishful thinking on the part of the bereaved who long to have the chance to say some sort of farewell to the person they love? Do they arise simply from a need for comfort? Are the dreams simply dreams with no import and no meaning? On the other hand, do dreams give us a clue about what happens when we die? Regardless of how a person answers these questions, near death experiences are helpful to some as they think about the afterlife.

Jeffrey Long, MD, is a radiation oncologist who is interested in near-death studies and research. Together with his wife, Jody, the two established the Near Death Experience Research Foundation. The non-profit's website (www.nderf.org) allows visitors a forum for expressing their own understanding of NDE. Those who are interested in NDE will find tons of information and testimonials on this website.

6.   It seems as if we are never satisfied. We always want more, especially of a good thing. Selfishness and selfcenteredness motivates much of what we do, say and believe. The "what's in it for me" attitude carries over into our religion and belief in a heaven.

I remember when Elaine and I, along with our young son, attended a birthday party for an eight-year-old. My son's friend had told his Dad, in no uncertain terms, that all he wanted for his birthday was a new bicycle. Instead of a guest bringing a present, which was the custom, each friend was to bring five dollars to go towards the purchase of a bicycle. After the games and enterainment had concluded, it was time for the traditional opening of presents. The father brought out a new bike. The boy's face was filled with delight. All of us went outside to watch the boy ride the new gift. After about five minutes, the boy stopped and indicated he was ready to open the rest of the gifts. The father informed him the bike was his only gift, as he had requested. The boy's face turned to disappointment. It was obvious he wanted and expected more. He was not satisfied with just one gift, even though it was what he requested.

We are not satisfied with the gift of life; we want more life. This can be expected from an immature child, but what about an adult? Am I being like a self-centered child by wanting more after I die?

Was it wrong for the little boy to expect more presents when he got what he asked for? Wanting more after we die may not be wrong. For me, it seems to be immature and selfish, rather than being grateful for what I have in this life. Is it possible to be both grateful and selfish? It is not only possible, but it is the nature of being human.

A person's belief is not invalid because he/she wants more in the afterlife. It is just that selfishness leads to all kinds of problems, while gratitude leaves us with joy and peace in the face of death. Being grateful for what I have even if there is nothing more, seems to be a more power-filled way to live my life and prepare for my death.

I have to ask myself whether this "what's in it for me" attitude really helps me prepare for death or gets in the way of living life to the fullest.

"What's in it for me" is not the message of Jesus. Is what God can do for us the main reason for believing? Is our worship a grateful response to God's gift of life or a way for getting something from God?

7.   I have not read how genetics plays a role in a person's belief in heaven. Nevertheless, I continue to wonder if our genetic makeup is a factor in determining what a person believes about the afterlife. Some studies indicate how we approach issues is affected by whether we are a right or left-brain person. I would love to read a doctoral thesis on the topic of how genetics influence our belief system.

8.   Although the Bible does not have a unified understanding of death, nevertheless, biblical passages influence what some people believe about the afterlife. The first century worldview of those who wrote the Bible reflects a three-storied universe, with heaven above the earth and hell below. This understanding shaped the writers' ideas about the afterlife and the language used to talk about their belief.

Many parts of the Bible address what happens in the afterlife. I agree with Professor Leander E. Keck. In the book, *Perspectives on Death,* he states, "The more clearly the milieu of the New Testament statements is perceived, the less possible it becomes to uproot them for instant theology or to combine them into a systematic treatment of the theology of death, resurrection, life after death, heaven, or hell. Rather than press the New Testament into a premature unity of thought, one should seek first to grasp its rich diversity, a diversity which reflects both the multifaceted tradition and the complex situation in which the literature was written . . ." (p. 94-95)

Yes, the Bible speaks about the afterlife, even though people of biblical times, like people in today's world, did not have the same understanding or way of expressing their belief.

Resurrection, salvation and faith are the words commonly used by the biblical writers when addressing the afterlife. Likewise, these three words refer to how God works in our daily life.

Growing up in the church, I was taught salvation referred to being saved from my sin. This meant I would receive the reward of heaven rather than the punishment of hell. Accepting Jesus as my Savior meant being forgiven for my sin. Without accepting this Savior I would not be saved and spend eternity in hell.

I have accepted Jesus as my Savior and this faith stance has nothing to do with the afterlife. Jesus' ministry and message saves me from my selfishness and greed. I continue to be a selfish rather than a giving person. My faith in Christ saves me from the guilt I feel when the self-centered part of me is working overtime. Salvation means being saved from a life dominated by getting. The forgiveness of God in Christ empowers me to be a more giving person. Salvation is when heaven is in us, not when we are in heaven. My relationship with Christ saves me, not for a future life, but for a fuller life in the here and now.

The truth of Christ saves me from loneliness. I have the assurance God's power is with me when I feel helpless and alone. I am saved from my fear, my fear of what others think and my fear of the unknown. The truth of God's grace, revealed in Christ, saves me from feeling my life has little value. I feel I am a person of worth and value, at least, to God.

Easter has been the big event for Christians. I was taught the resurrection of Jesus assured me of living eternally in heaven. I, too, would rise from the dead.

My belief in the resurrection of Jesus is unrelated to the afterlife. The truth and meanings of the death of Christ bring new life to me. When I feel dead because of life circumstances, I become alive by connecting with Jesus. New life becomes mine when I unite myself to the life, death and resurrection of Jesus. Resurrection means Christ is alive in the life and spirit of many people, including myself.

For many, the word *faith* refers to their belief in eternal life. My faith focuses on what is, rather than what will be. For me, faith is responding to the truth that God will guide, direct and empower me as I live my life.

Paul states the central truth of the Christian faith: "We are justified by faith." The word "justified" means united with, connected to, in close relationship with. Faith connects us with God. We come into a close relationship with God through faith in Christ.

Ten lepers approached Jesus asking him to have mercy on them. All ten were cleansed. (Luke 17:14) Only one expressed gratitude to God. Jesus said to him, "Rise and go your way; your faith has made you well." For Jesus, faith is responding with gratitude to God for the gift of life.

A man asked Jesus what he should do to inherit eternal life. Jesus responded with a story (Luke 10:25-37) about how God wants us to live life in the spirit of love and righteousness. Faith is gratefully living life in the spirit of love.

What happens after I die is not important or relevant in my preparation for death. What happens before I die is important. Because heaven is clothed in mystery, I choose to focus on how God's grace empowers our daily life.

Dexter was a member of our congregation and a regular worshipper. Over the years, he heard me preach approximiately 500 sermons. One day he said to me, "I remember you telling me several years ago that you do not know what happens after we die. But, don't you have something to offer to the subject? What do you believe about the afterlife?" I said to him, "How many of the sermons you heard me preach dealt with heaven?" "Yes, your sermons were about how God fits into our everyday life," responded Dexter. "Does that mean you don't have a belief in heaven?" "I have a belief," I assured him. "It's just that how Jesus empowers me to live my daily life with God is more important to me than what God has in store for me after I die. In fact," I continued, "if there were nothing more for me after I die I would still be a devoted believer. If there is more, it is simply a bonus. Frankly, I would love to see my loved ones after I die. If there is more, I welcome it with joy. If there is nothing more after I die, I am grateful for the gift I undeservingly have received. I do not need the bonus of my life continuing after I die in order to have faith in God and live thankfully for the love God offers each moment of my life."

There is great amount of pain in people's lives and the world. Directing our energy and time to how God works in our daily lives is more productive than speculating how God works after we die. When it comes to matters of faith, making this world more humane and loving calls for our undivided attention.

Imagine mowing your lawn. Suddenly, you see smoke and flames emerging from the windows of your house. With a sense of urgency, you fly into action. In order that the house and people's lives are not destroyed, you do all you can to put out the fire.

The fires of hate, selfishness, greed, loneliness, fear and injustice are raging every day. Does concern about a fire in the afterlife distract people from the all-important task of dealing aggressively with the fires that daily threaten to destroy people's lives and the world?

When I was attending seminary, as part of the training, I witnessed an autopsy in a local hospital. I watched (as much as I would let myself look at what I considered a gross process) as the doctor dissected and disassembled the person's body parts. After the autopsy was completed, the doctor gathered up the body parts, put them in a plastic bag and returned them to the body. The chest flaps were then closed and sewn back together.

In conversation with the doctor who did the procedure, we learned he was a Christian fundamentalist. His belief in the afterlife was considerably different from my belief. After watching the autopsy I asked him, "How can you believe that in the afterlife our bodies will continue in the form they are in this life?" He responded by saying, "I have faith that if God could put our bodies together in the miraculous form they are now, surely he can take what I have done in the autopsy and put the body parts back together again in the final resurrection."

Although I do not share the doctor's understanding of what happens after we die, what a person believes about the afterlife does not mean his/her ideas are right or wrong, valid or invalid. What happens after we die is clouded in mystery. Therefore, it does not make sense to contend that a person's understanding of what happens in life after death is correct or incorrect.

I believe God's grace is sufficient unto every need. I believe we have all we can handle in figuring out how to make this life more grace-filled. God in Christ gives meaning and purpose to a person's life. I do not know what happens after I die. Therefore, it is important to focus on what we do know. God knows the world and people's lives need the message of grace proclaimed with clarity and vigor.

In his classic poem, *A Psalm of Life*, Henry Wadsworth Longfellow's focus is on living this life to the fullest. Another reason for quoting this poem is because I memorized it when I was in the sixth grade. My grade school teacher challenged the class to learn this poem and I accepted the challenge.

Tell me not, in mournful numbers,
Life is but an empty dream!—
For the soul is dead that slumbers,
And things are not what they seem.

Life is real! Life is earnest!
And the grave is not its goal;
Dust thou art, to dust returnest,
Was not spoken of the soul.

Not enjoyment, and not sorrow,
Is our destined end or way;
But to act, that each to-morrow
Find us farther than to-day.

Art is long, and Time is fleeting,
And our hearts, though stout and brave,
Still, like muffled drums, are beating
Funeral marches to the grave.

In the world's broad field of battle,
In the bivouac of Life,
Be not like dumb, driven cattle!
Be a hero in the strife!

Trust no Future, howe'er pleasant!
Let the dead Past bury its dead!
Act,—act in the living Present!
Heart within, and God o'erhead!

Lives of great men all remind us
We can make our lives sublime,
And, departing, leave behind us
Footprints on the sands of time;

Footprints, that perhaps another,
Sailing o'er life's solemn main,
A forlorn and shipwrecked brother,
Seeing, shall take heart again.

Let us, then, be up and doing,
With a heart for any fate;
Still achieving, still pursuing,
Learn to labor and to wait.

It may feel peculiar to consider that a Christian pastor would think heaven is irrelevant for his preparation for death, especially since the majority of Christians believe in heaven.

Throughout my ministry I have been reluctant to talk about the afterlife. This is because my belief is different from what most people were taught to believe. I did not want to offend people for whom heaven is the cornerstone of their belief.

There are times I wish I could believe my life will continue as it is this present moment. I am not scared of dying. I am scared of not living, not being able to see, touch, smell, hear and love. I would like to believe that I will be reunited with my mother and father in heaven. However, I continue to question whether this will happen and I am okay with my uncertainty about heaven.

After I shared with Dexter how focusing on this life is more important to me than the afterlife, he said, "I get it, but I still want to know what you believe about the afterlife." "Ok," I said, "but before I give you my ideas it is important to understand I do not contend my ideas are right and others are wrong. Many people believe very differently than I do about heaven and eternal life. There are sufficient verses of Scripture about heaven and the afterlife to support any idea a person may have, if that is how they choose to use the Bible. But, you asked, so I will give you what I've got. While my beliefs are still being formulated, nevertheless, I enjoy discussing the afterlife with folks.

"I believe mystery reigns over this ultimate question about life after death. Obviously, I do not know what happens after we die. Simply stated, here is what I believe. I believe after I die, I will be with God. 'Whether we live or die, we belong to God.' (Romans 14:7, 8)

"Are you disappointed? Did you expect and want more? There are rare moments when I desire more clarity for my belief in the afterlife. However, most of the time I am content with my belief. Focusing how God is at work in my daily life is sufficient. I will leave the afterlife to God."

Now that I have stated my brief credo about the afterlife, let me go a step further and explain three things I mean when I say I will belong to God after I die.

1. For me, love is the most helpful word for understanding who God is and how God works. When I do acts of love, especially unconditional love, my love becomes part of God and lives on eternally. I find consolation knowing the love I have given throughout my lifetime will continue after I die. One hundred years from now and beyond, people will believe in God. The love you and I give to others becomes part of God as soon as we give it. Once God has received our love, we begin living eternally.

Moses, Paul, Gandhi, Martin Luther King and others in your life, whom you can name, have made significant contributions to our life today. They reveal to us the power of God. They live today. As we contribute to doing God's will, we, too, make our contribution to making this a better world. This contribution lives on after we die. It lives on in the life of God and God never dies.

2. When you acknowledge you are made in God's image, you own the spark of divinity within you. As you decide to transform that spark into fire by giving back in whatever way you choose and fits your gifts, you add to the life of God. You and your gifts live on forever. Neither sin nor death can take it away. Once you give back to another, once you love another, once you give your gifts to another, they become forever part of the divine energy. When someone draws strength/power/wisdom/truth from God, you are part of the process that lives eternally.

3. Creator is another word that is helpful in clarifying who God is and how God works. When I use my creativity to build a more godlike world, I contribute to the ongoing reality of God. God uses for good my creative achievements. My accomplishments live on forever as those who follow me participate in God's power and presence.

In a profound sense, there can be no end to my love and creativity. God, who has accepted, received and responded to my love and creativity, is the One for whom there is neither beginning nor end. Joy and comfort come from knowing I will be forever part of God's purposes. As my gifts live on in others and thus in God, I feel assured of having eternal life.

This may not be enough for you. It is sufficient for me. Indeed, it is comforting to ponder how I will live on in the life of God's love forever. Reflecting upon the small ways I have contributed to the life and spirit of others, I feel at ease. My life lives on as God imparts power and grace to everyone who is yet unborn.

4.   I do not believe our human bodies continue after we die. Nevertheless, I find myself believing something more continues to exist besides our bodies.

Humans have always looked for ways to talk about what they cannot see or touch. Down through history, "soul" seems to be the most popular word to talk about what happens after we die. Many consider the soul to be a part of our physical bodies as much as our heart or lungs.

Greek philosophers, such as Plato and Socrates, spoke about the immortality of the soul. Plato sets forth the idea that only the body is mortal. The soul, the essence of a person, lives on after death. In Plato's classic formulation, a human has an immortal soul. For the Greeks the body was a prison and death was a friend. In death the soul is set free from the physical body that holds a person prisoner. Socrates says that just as snow cannot be warm, or fire cold; so the soul, which bears and brings life, cannot be dead.

The Bible views life as good and death is not a friend, but rather an enemy to be overcome. Living life as a good gift rather than a prison, contains more hope for making life what God intends.

Many today, including Christians, believe after we die our soul continues to live. In I Corinthians 15:44, Paul refers to a "spiritual body" being raised after death. There are Christian theologians and writers who point out the Greek idea of the immortality of the soul and the New Testament idea of the resurrection of a spiritual body are not the same. Personally, I find the distinction adds little to understand the afterlife. I have yet to come across a clear and understandable definition of "soul" or "spiritual body". Therefore, I find both terms of little help in knowing what happens after we die.

I find myself thinking there is more after we die, even if I have no clue about the nature of that "more". I tend to believe if I can see and touch something then it is real. I got a D+ in high school physics and that was because of the teacher's generosity. I avoided chemistry. I have a mental block when someone talks about things that exist which I cannot see, such as molecules, atoms, protons, gravity, travel of light, etc. Yet, I know much exists in the cosmos that we cannot see or know.

Therefore, I believe there may be another form of existence after this earthly body dies. To a person like me, the difference between a living and dead body is the living body is active and a dead body is latent. When the body is extent and latent, the molecules obey a superior attraction which draws them asunder and scatters them through space. The dispersion is death, if it is possible to conceive such a thing as death where the very molecules of the dead body manifest an intense, vital energy.

Somewhere I read the following; "The atom is but a collection of elementary particles, the molecule a collection of atoms, proteins a construct of amino-acid molecules, the cell a shrewd mixture of fat, sugar, and protein, the living organism nothing but a tissue of cells. In the end humans seems to be little more than an immense molecule, the most complex of all, but a molecule just the same." Who knows, I may become a molecule and in two years or two hundred years be resurrected in another human body.

5.   My experience of life reveals death is just one part of a cyclic process of birth, death and rebirth. Death is not the end of a cycle. The leaves fall off the trees and it is not the end. They go back to the soil, nourish the roots and next year the tree has new leaves. This same dynamic of rebirth happens to humans who are part of nature. According to these principles, death is a change of form, an imperceptible passage from one existence into another.

Every winter I look out my window at the trees that appear dead. Every spring I see resurrection. I see the rebirth of what once was death. Does my dead body add to nature's compost heap, becoming the manure without which nothing more arises? In death, do I become part of a never-ending process of death and life? The most revealing evidence of this phenomenon of life comes as we witness how a dying caterpillar gives new life to a butterfly.

There are those who say if this life is it and there is nothing after we die, life is meaningless. Is cake worthless without icing? Is pie nothing without ice cream? I love cake without icing and enjoy pie without ice cream. I also love and enjoy life even if there is nothing more after I die.

I am not under any illusion that my ideas about the afterlife are correct or even helpful to you. They simply are mine. I hope they contribute in some small way to the dialogue about what happens after we die. Meanwhile, I am content to know I will be part of God and the God-experience forever.

QUESTIONS FOR CONTEMPLATION AND DISCUSSION

1. What were you taught about the afterlife? What part still makes sense and what part have you rejected and/or altered?
2. The author goes to great length to repudiate the reward aspect of the afterlife. Why do you agree or disagree?
3. Is knowing you will be with God after you die sufficient to your faith, or do you want/need more? Why? Why not?
4. The author is content to focus on how God is at work in this life and leave the afterlife a mystery. How do you respond to this perspective?
5. Has this book changed your ideas/beliefs in the afterlife? Why? Why not?

7

ALWAYS CARRY TWO STONES

Recently, I voted in the presidential election. It took me five minutes to vote. In some states, people stood in line for over three hours. As these people were preparing to vote, I suspect some wondered whether it was worth it. After all, would their one vote really make a difference? Undoubtedly, some stepped out of line and went home. Many believed their vote counted and remained in line.

Was my vote important? Did my vote make a difference? The answer is yes and no. For me, this is a paradox.

No, President Obama would still be President even if I stayed home. My vote is even more unimportant in light of the fact I live in a red state. The Electoral College system makes my one vote irrelevant.

Yes, my vote is important. By voting, I expressed my gratitude for living in this great country. My vote is a testimony to my decision to be a responsible citizen. What if everyone decided his/her vote did not matter? Our democratic system would disintegrate. My vote ensures good things will continue for others and me.

Over the years, literature, philosophy and theology frequently communicated truth by the use of paradox. A paradox is a seemingly absurd or self-contradictory statement or proposition that when investigated or explained may prove to be well-founded or true. The intent of a paradox is not to mislead, but rather lead us into deeper understanding. A paradox may seem at first like a contradiction, but it turns out to be a resourceful blending of opposites.

In a paradox, the two conflicting elements would seem to cancel each other. After all, nothing can be both true and false at the same time and still be true. However, when we look at a magnetic field we find in physics a veritable paradox. Indeed, for a magnetic field to exist, both negative and positive opposites must exist. A magnetic field both attracts and repels. When we encounter a paradox, our attention is directed to contrary elements. We ponder two truths in a fresh way. Heads and tails on a dime look different, but both are part of the same coin. Sometimes the truth, like the coin, shows two different faces.

The Chinese philosophy of "yin and yang" literally means "shadow and light." Yin and yang describe how polar opposites or seemingly contrary forces are interconnected and interdependent. Yin and yang are not opposing forces, but complementary forces that interact to form a greater whole.

I find paradox to be more than a literary device. A paradox is not just a witty or amusing statement. A paradox holds serious implications for those who seek understanding when life is confusing and troubling. A paradox clarifies the meaning when life is disconcerting and difficult.

The Bible's frequent use of paradox helps us prepare for living and dying. Scripture demonstrates how much of our faith is paradoxical. For example, Paul states, "Strength is made perfect in weakness." (I Corinthians 12:9) "When I am weak, then I am strong." (II Corinthians 12:10)

Jesus often meets a situation with a story instead of an explanation. Instead of a simple statement, he gives us a paradox. Jesus said, "I come not to bring peace but a sword." (Matthew 10:34) "The one who would be greatest must be servant." (Matthew 23:11) "Blessed are the meek for they will inherit the earth." (Matthew 5:5) "Those who lose their life will find it." (Luke 17:33) "Enter through the narrow gate. For wide is the gate and broad is the road that leads to destruction, and many enter through it. But small is the gate and narrow the road that leads to life and only a few find it."(Matthew 7:13, 14)

John Dominic Crossan, a New Testament scholar, points out how many of "the parables of Jesus are paradoxical, a deliberate 'polar reversal' of the expected narrative plot. The function of Jesus' paradoxes is to challenge people's self-evident façade of worldly wisdom. Jesus' use of paradox directs us to a different understanding of truth from our normal or habitual ways of thinking and acting. As a parable incorporates paradox, a radical truth unfolds that exceeds the grasp of conventional logic and eludes the reach of our demands for objective certainty. Through the paradox, we are put on the spot and left exposed and vulnerable before truth that insists on a response."

In the parable of the prodigal son (Luke 14:11-32), we are invited into the life of a wayward son who receives the unconditional love of the father. The father accepts the younger son home from his life of rebellion and corrupt living and celebrates with a party. The obedient and faithful older son became jealous and resentful, the root cause of his estrangement from the father's love. While the younger son appears to be on the outside in self-imposed exile, he is on the inside of the father's grace. While the older son appears to be on the inside in loyalty to his father, he becomes on the outside in self-imposed alienation.

The title of the parable in Luke 10:25-37 is itself a paradox. In Palestine, "good" was not a term used to describe a Samaritan. They were considered outcast, outsiders and unrighteous. To call a Samaritan "good" would be like speaking of a good louse. The Jewish priest and Levite, who many considered agents of holiness and divine favor, are viewed with religious scorn as they pass by a person needing love and compassion. The Samaritan, who is the object of socio-religious scorn, is the agent of love and divine favor. With the use of paradox, Jesus drove home the truth as to the qualities of a truly religious person.

The following paradox has helped me prepare for death: we are important and, at the same time, we are unimportant. Both statements are true and each has its value. Each brings meaning and purpose to life and death.

Look closer at each aspect of this paradox and discover the truths that empower us to live and die with hope.

I.   We are unimportant. I am important to my family, a few friends and possibly a number of other people. At the same time, if I were to die tomorrow, these people would grieve for a period; *and* life would continue.

We can verify and understand our unimportance by exploring the mystery and vastness of the universe.

The new Hubble Space telescope has observed 3,000 visible galaxies. This is twice the number observed before with the old camera. The most distant galaxies are 13.2 billion light-years from Earth, meaning their light has taken 13.2 billion years to travel to Hubble's cameras. The word, visible, is significant because with radio telescopes and infrared cameras, other galaxies undetected by Hubble are being identified. It is estimated there are 125 billion galaxies in the universe. As observations continue and astronomers explore more of our universe, the number of galaxies discovered will increase.

Add up all the galaxies in the entire universe and the number of galaxies could be in the trillions. It is mind boggling how many galaxies could be out there. Many of us wonder how many habitable planets there are in the many galaxies.

Scientists estimate the universe in which we live is between thirteen and fourteen billion years old. The planet earth, a tiny part of that universe, is between four and five billion years old. No living thing, however, appeared on this planet until about a hundred million years after earth came into being. Human life, depending on what definition is used for that life, did not arrive on this planet until somewhere between two million and one hundred thousand years ago. Equating the appearance of life on the planet earth to 24 hours, modern human species arrived on the scene about 11:58 p.m. The known history of the world, that is the establishment of empires, founding of religions, art, music and science, took place in the last two tenths of a second.

The number of years I have spent on this earth is less than a fraction of a second. Before August 21, 1939, I was not important. I did not exist. I have zero anxious feelings about not experiencing the innumerable events that took place before I was born. Why would I have anxious feelings about not experiencing the innumerable events that will take place when my brief life on this earth is over? Being dead will be no different from being unborn. I was unimportant then and I shall be unimportant after I die.

In the face of the unfathomable reality of space and time, the planet earth is just a speck. And in light of knowing I am one of seven billion people living on this speck for an infinitesimal amount of time, how important is my one life? I am less than a speck, maybe just a molecule.

The phrase "earth to earth, ashes to ashes, dust to dust" is often used in funeral liturgy. The phrase is from the Book of Common Prayer. The words are inspired by Genesis 3:19: "By the sweat of your brow you will eat your food until you return to the ground, since from it you were taken; for dust you are and to dust you will return."

Psalm 90 reminds us of the transitory nature of life. "Lord, you have been our dwelling place throughout all generations. Before the mountains were born or you brought forth the whole world, from everlasting to everlasting you are God. You turn people back to dust, saying, 'Return to dust, you mortals.' A thousand years in your sight are like a day that has just gone by or like a watch in the night. Yet you sweep people away in the sleep of death. They are like the new grass of the morning. In the morning it springs up new, but by evening it is dry and withered . . . . Our days may come to seventy years, or eighty."

Is this pessimism or are the biblical writers helping us face reality, teaching us "to number our days that we may gain a heart of wisdom," (Psalm 90) and reminding us "to dust you will return."

For reasons I have yet to understand fully, some of the sting of death is eased when I accept my unimportance. When I understand my unimportance, I refrain from taking myself too seriously. This is a positive thing, for at least five reasons.

First, by taking myself too seriously, I become mired in trivia and non-essentials. I fail to focus on what is important in life. As I reflect on my life, I think of all the stupid and unhealthy things I said and did because I took myself too seriously. To affirm my unimportance keeps my life in proper perspective. It enables me to major in majors rather than majoring in minors. I find myself better able to live by the slogan, "Don't sweat the small stuff."

Second, taking myself too seriously increases self-absorption and self-centeredness. Worry and stress comes from preoccupation with our own welfare. I worry less when I refrain from taking myself too seriously. My stress level increases when I allow myself to think I am more important than I am.

Third, by taking myself too seriously I become closed to the opinions and ideas of others. I fail to be objective, keep things in proper perspective and look at the big picture. People who are judgmental and critical take themselves too seriously.

Fourth, much of our unhappiness come from attempting to validate our importance by trying to live up to what others think is important for us to accomplish. Acknowledging our unimportance enables us to avoid the erroneous and dangerous philosophy that contends a person's importance is based on wealth, position, education and outward appearance. We will spend less time striving for position and power.

Fifth, the chances for becoming a workaholic are increased when we take ourselves too seriously. Hard work is admirable and good, unless it gets in the way of treasuring the simple beauties of life.

All of these five life experiences increase anxiety. Be serious about who you are and what you do, but don't take yourself too seriously.

Bette Davis said, "I don't take the movies seriously and anyone who does is in for a headache." Many have unnecessary headaches as the result of taking themselvs too seriously.

People who understand the truths of the unimportant side of the paradox are humble. Humility is a powerful tool for facing the realities of life. Jesus used paradoxes to lift up the power of humility. "The first shall be last and the last first." (Matthew 26:16) "Those who lose their life will find it."(Matthew 16:25) Humility is a virtue, the seed that produces good fruit and meaning in life.

I recall numerous times throughout my lifetime when an event happened which at the time I thought was very important. Now, as I look back on that event, it seems insignificant and unimportant.

I thought my life was over when I did not play one minute in an important basketball game. My college team, Wichita State, was playing the number one team in the nation, Cincinnati Bearcats. Their All-American, Oscar Robertson, was one of the best basketball players ever to play in the NBA. It was my junior year. As a sophomore, I was the starting guard and played almost all of the two games we played against Cincinnati. That year, they were number two in the nation, behind Ohio State who had such greats as John Havlicek and Jerry Lucas. (They beat us by seven points that year) As a sophomore and junior, I started every game and played approximately 90 percent of the time. One important game against Cincinnati, in an effort to knock off the number one team, the coach decided on a different lineup. Thus, I did not play. I was devastated. I was depressed. I was focused on myself and not the team. The most important game of the year and I was on the bench. Now, as I look back on the event, I am certain I was the only person aware of this event or cared about it. Even at the time, it was not as important as I made it out to be.

The awareness of my death puts things in proper perspective. Frequently, what I think is important is unimportant. I now realize true importance is what is important to God. I am sure God was not interested in my "important" event of not getting to play in the game. As I look back on those events, they were simply times when my self-centeredness was working overtime. In hindsight, I realize they were not important to God. The only events that are truly important are those events that are important to God.

I remember my grandparents. I have no memory of my great grandparents. I do not know whether a distant ancestor was a good or bad individual. Were they loving? Did they succeed? I do not know and am unmoved to find out. They are forgotten. Each of us faces the same future. We, too, will be forgotten. No matter how important I think I am, the world will get along without me, as it did before my birth. Keeping our importance in proper perspective grows spiritual, emotional and physical health.

On the day I die, I will be one of approximately 155,000 people who die each day. In light of the awesome span of history, our life is not important. If my life were to end prematurely, I would become part of God. As far as history is concerned, I will be forgotten. This reality can lead to futility and hopelessness or it can add meaning and purpose to each day.

Ernest Becker writes, "Man is literally split in two: he has awareness of his own splendid uniqueness in that he sticks out of nature with a towering majesty, and yet he goes back into the ground a few feet in order blindly and dumbly to rot and disappear forever."

We prepare for death in a healthy manner by keeping the level of our importance in proper perspective.

II. Powerful and good things happen when I affirm the flip side of the paradox. We are important. Accepting our importance becomes a driving force for making this a better world. God needs our gifts to build a more humane and loving world.

People, who know how important they are to God, live with meaning and purpose. "Therefore, I say to you, do not worry about your life, what you will eat or what you will drink; nor about your body, what you will put on. Is not life more than food and the body more than clothing? Look at the birds of the air, for they neither sow nor reap nor gather into barns; yet your God feeds them. Are you not more important than they?" (Matthew 6:25, 26)

People who see themselves as important have a positive self-image. They accept themselves, warts and all. Consequently, they acknowledge every human being is made in the image of God. Loving others becomes a lifestyle. Love and understanding toward others flow and grow as the result of affirming our importance to God.

I have decided not only am I important, I am chosen. The Old and New Testaments refer to God choosing a people for a divine purpose. Some elements of religion, including Muslim, Judaism and Christianity, interpret "chosen" as being better, superior and privileged. Some even go so far as to believe that being chosen means their religion is the only true religion; and if you do not believe as they believe, you will not go to heaven. Certainly, I do not think I am chosen because of my good works. Being chosen and receiving grace are synonymous.

I am chosen in the true biblical sense. God has chosen you and me to make this a better world. People who believe they are chosen and important are motivated to make their lives count and increase love and understanding among all peoples of the earth.

Affirming our importance comes from three primary sources.

First, we are made in the image of God. (Genesis 1:26) Just as God creates, so we humans have the capacity to create. Just as God loves, so we humans have the ability to love. Just as God is important, because we are made in God's image we, therefore, are important.

Second, you are important because you are important to God. No matter what you have done or left undone, you are important to God. You may have failed to live up to what you expected of yourself. A relationship may have gone sour because of your actions and attitude. No matter what you have experienced in life, you are important to God. This unconditional love is the nature of God and the essence of the Gospel. Those who accept this good news, this grace, find life fulfilling.

Third, accepting your importance is the only lifestyle that makes sense. I cringe to think what this world and my life would be like without those significant people in my life who decided their life was important. The purpose and direction I have experienced in my life would not be the same without Sue and Mildred, two homemakers in a small Kansas town, who took their job as youth sponsors seriously. In the vastness of time and space, they were just a speck. To me, they were God's representatives.

It is helpful to distinguish between *feeling* you are important and *knowing* you are important. Those who *feel* important are arrogant and self-centered. Even their motivation for doing good arises from a need to be important. They define importance by whether they live up to how others define importance. Feeling important is dependent upon what is accomplished and achieved. Winning and wealth are necessary in order to feel important. Low self-esteem accompanies this attitude.

People who *know* they are important refrain from defining their importance by what they do or do not accomplish. Affirming their importance is not tied to being better than someone or having more wealth. Their self-esteem is high and growing. People who know they are important have connected with the unconditional love (grace) of God.

People who *feel* important do weird things in order to validate their importance. Those who *know* they are important humbly realize their importance is ultimately a gift.

Are you and I indispensable? The answer is yes and no. Yes, you are indispensable. There is no other person like you with your unique gifts and talents. God needs your special and unique gifts. Paradoxically, no one is indispensable. God will bring forth others who will take our place and continue building a better world. Embracing the totality of this paradox is essential, lest our importance becomes a source of

egotism and self-centeredness and our insignificance leads to futility
and discouragement.

Isaac Watts expressed this truth in the familiar hymn, *O God Our Help in Ages Past.*

O God, our help in ages past, our hope for years to come,
Our shelter from the stormy blast, and our eternal home.
Under the shadow of thy throne, still may we dwell secure;
Sufficient is thine arm alone, and our defense is sure.

A thousand ages, in thy sight, are like an evening gone;
Short as the watch that ends the night, before the rising sun.
Time, like an ever-rolling stream, bears all who breathe away;
They fly forgotten, as a dream dies at the opening day.

Last night, as I was going to sleep, I had the thought: what if I
die in my sleep. Ever so often, I have this thought and I realize how
unimportant my life is. There will be some grief, but life will go on
as if I had never lived. At the same time, if I don't die in my sleep, it
is crucial that I realize my life is important to God and God's work.
Conclusion: I am unimportant and I am important. Living with the
paradox is helpful for facing my mortality.

Several years ago, a friend of mine was talking about how, in
reference to a particular event in his life, part of him felt sad and part of
him felt happy. Understanding there are several parts of me is helpful
for accepting others and myself. For example, part of me knows I am
very important and part of me knows I am not all that important. Part
of me realizes what I do is important and my death will have an impact
upon others. Another part of me realizes I am one small particle of sand
in a massive beach, and my death will have very few consequences in
the whole realm of things.

If I die tomorrow, 99.9% plus of the people living will not even
know about the event. The world will continue as if I never existed.
When I think of my ashes being poured into a lake or onto a golf course
or . . . . , I realize how unimportant and insignificant my life has been.
Yet, had I not given my gifts and lived as if my life were important,

some people's lives would not be as full and rich as they are. I truly believe the world is a wee bit better because I decided my life was important, at least to God. When we live and die knowing our life is important to God, the number of people who are enriched by our love is multiplied infinitely.

An old rabbinic saying admonishes us to keep two stones in our picket. One stone is inscribed with the words, "I am but dust and aches," and the other stone, "For my sake was the world created." Possessing these two stones prepares us to face our death with style and grace.

The truth of this paradox is powerfully clarified in the biblical book of Ecclesiastes.

QUESTIONS FOR CONTEMPLATION AND DISCUSSION

1. How do you respond to the idea that your life is unimportant? Does it lessen your death anxiety? Why? Why not?

2. How do you respond to the idea that your life is important? Does it lessen your death anxiety? Why? Why not?

3. In what way does God speak to you by using paradox in the Bible?

4. How do you understand the author's distinction between *feeling* you are unimportant/important and *knowing* you are unimportant/important?

8

HOW TO LIVE AS A PESSIMISTIC OPTIMIST

Throughout Ecclesiastes, grace and truth are communicated by the use of paradox. The book begins by proclaiming that all is vanity. We are unimportant. This is countered with the affirmation that all of life is a gift from God. We are important. The author records these contraries without choosing between them.

Many readers of Ecclesiastes contend it is a negative book. This would be the view of people who subscribe to the power of positive thinking philosophy. They believe it is best to avoid negative thoughts and feelings by focusing only on the positive.

Everyone experiences doubt, fear, anger and anxiety. We deprive ourselves of great opportunities when we strive to quash these mental states by the "power of positive thinking." It is healthier to face, investigate and learn from our experiences.

To live knowing you are important is a positive experience and affords power for living and dying. To live knowing you are unimportant is also a positive experience and provides power for living and dying.

Living this paradox enables people to shift gears. They are able to balance striving for success and security with openness to failure and uncertainty. They tolerate tension better and manage the ambiguities of life that frequently come our way. The ability to recognize the ebb and flow of life is a key to healthy living. This is especially true when it comes to affirming that we are important and unimportant.

The author of Ecclesiastes is a walking contradiction, exactly like many of us. This ancient book refuses to accept easy answers about life. Ecclesiastes is comforting to those of us who have questions about what we believe. Through this book of the Bible, God gives me permission to accept thoughts and feelings that often are paradoxical. As the author expressed his pessimism about life, he droped optimism into the mix.

I have always seen myself as a doubting believer and a pessimistic optimist. I am a hopeful fatalist and a secular spiritualist. This is the Ecclesiastes approach to life and faith.

Ecclesiastes receives its name from the Septuagint, the Greek translation of the Old Testament. In the Septuagint, the book is called *ekklesiastes*, a word that means "assembly, congregation." The name of the book in Hebrew is "Qoheleth," coming from the word "qahal," and means "one who assembles." "Qoheleth" is commonly referred to as the author of Ecclesiastes. Because Qoheleth is identified as "the son of David, king in Jerusalem" (1:1), by implication the Book of Ecclesiastes has been traditionally ascribed to the Israelite King Solomon.

The Hebrew word for vanity is "hebel", which occurs 37 times in Ecclesiastes. The New International Version translates hebel as "meaningless", and the Good News Bible as "useless". Some commentaries view vanity as negative and pessimistic. The literal meaning of hebel, "breath" or "vapor," serves as a multi-layered symbol for the author's analysis of life in the human realm.

The author is not saying that life is vain or meaningless—so grab for whatever fun you can find. Rather, he uses hebel to describe a world of tragedy and chance, in which good things are short-lived and where treasured things turn out to be of little worth. Although this is certainly grim, the author has not given up hope. He advises his readers how to make the most of their lives in the midst of such realities.

Qoheleth is saying life is transitory. We are here today and gone tomorrow. "What has been will be again. What has been done will be done again; there is nothing new under the sun." (1:9) The people of long ago are not remembered, nor will there be any remembrance of people yet to come by those who come after them." (1:11) We are unimportant.

All is vanity. All things in life lack ultimate importance. The author is identifying a sense of frustration that is fundamental to our relationship with the world in which we live. In Ecclesiastes, the image that often accompanies the idea of vanity is "chasing after wind."

Webster's dictionary definition of vanity points to the word "vain." When someone is vain, he/she is self-absorbed and egotistical. They possess an exaggerated sense of their self-importance. A vain person is self-satisfied. People who are vain lack substance. Humility is not a major motivating force in their lives.

When Ecclesiastes speaks of vanity, our human limitations are acknowledged. "All have sinned and fallen short of the glory of God." (Romans 3:23) These words hold value and truth. Recognizing the limitations of our knowledge and power opens us to receive the wisdom and power of God. We are more inclined to accept our strengths. In this obscure and frequently ignored book of the Old Testament, we find the central truth of the New Testament: we are justified not by works of the law, but by the gift of God, which is faith.

As the author of Ecclesiastes experiences the vanity aspects of life, he simultaneously experiences God. Ecclesiastes shows us a man who lives in a world of "vanity" and comes out on the other side with a wiser, more seasoned perspective. When we are surrounded by the temptation to proclaim life's ultimate emptiness, we can find in Ecclesiastes a vision tempered by experience and ultimately seen through divinely colored lenses. Life is destined to remain unsatisfying apart from our recognition of God's intervention and grace.

Understanding "all is vanity" opens us to the other side of the paradox: "All is given by God." (2:1) Grace fills the book of Ecclesiastes. Vanity focuses on what is temporary, impermanent and transitory. The opposite side of Qoheleth's paradox focuses on what is lasting, permanent and enduring, words that point us to the nature of God. "I know that whatever God does endures forever; nothing can be added to it, nor anything taken from it. God has made it so." (3:14)

The reading Ecclesiastes invites us into a God-centered world view while accepting the unknowable aspects of life and God. "God has made everything suitable for its time; moreover God has put a sense of past and future into their minds, yet they cannot find out what God has done from the beginning to the end." (3:11) "When I applied my mind to know wisdom, and to see the business that is done on earth, how one's eyes see sleep neither day nor night, then I saw all the work of God, that no one can find out what is happening under the sun. However much they may toil in seeking, they will not find it out; even though those who are wise claim to know, they cannot find it out."(8:16, 17)

In Ecclesiastes, we see the author debating with himself, torn between what he cannot help seeing and what he cannot help believing. Rather than staying stuck in the vanity part of life, Qoheleth directs us to the God part of life. "Remember your creator in the days of your youth." (12:1) Life in the world has significance when we remember our Creator, even when we experience life as vanity.

By accepting the vanity aspect of life, we are driven to accept God's role in our vanity experiences. As we try to make sense of what often feels like a senseless world (vanity), we turn to find meaning in the reality of God.

Ecclesiastes concludes by admonishing the reader to fear God. "The end of the matter; all has been heard. Fear God, and keep the commandments; for that is the whole duty of everyone. For God will bring every deed into judgment, including every secret thing, whether good or evil."(12:13)

Throughout the Bible, the mystery of God is proclaimed in the phrase, "fear God." Fear does not mean dread or fright about God and/ or the future. Rather, fear is best translated with words such as respect, reverence and awe. "The fear of God is the beginning of knowledge." (Proverbs 1:7)

As Qoheleth speaks of a God who is veiled in mystery, he also proclaims, "God has made everything beautiful in its time. God has set eternity in our hearts." (3:11) Again, a paradox: God is unknowable and lives within us. We are important.

Respect for the mystery of God has always been an important tenet of my faith. God is not absent; God is simply beyond all my attempts to domesticate the Divine. The world is filled with paradox and mystery. I find peace as I rest in the God beyond words. Where there is no mystery, there is no challenge, nor a place for imagination to flourish. Albert Einstein said, "The most beautiful experience we can have is the mysterious—the fundamental emotion which stands at the cradle of true art and true science."

In the midst of vanity, Qoheleth invites the reader to enjoy each moment of life. If you find Ecclesiastes pessimistic, you missed the numerous joyful passages of this ancient book. "There is nothing better for mortals than to eat and drink, and find enjoyment in their toil. This also, I saw, is from the hand of God." (2:24) "This is what I have seen to be good: it is fitting to eat and drink and find enjoyment in all the toil with which one toils under the sun the few days of the life God gives us; for this is our lot." (5:18) "So I commend enjoyment, for there is nothing better for people under the sun than to eat, drink and enjoy themselves, for this will go with them in their toil through the days of life that God gives them under the sun." (8:15) "Go, eat your bread with enjoyment, and drink your wine with a merry heart; for God has long ago approved what you do." (9:11)

The advice might sound hedonistic, until it is married to the truth that all life is a gift from God. Qoheleth insists, often in the same passage, that life is filled with both vanity and joy. Ecclesiastes provides a balance for the frequent meaningless experiences of life while underscoring Qoheleth's conviction that there is joy in life. The overall effect of this close juxtaposition of passages about *hebel* and exhortations to joy is to reveal that where the meaning of life has eluded us, even then, we can decide to find joy in the good things of life.

The message of Ecclesiastes is inspired by the author's recognition that "death is the destiny of every man; the living should take this to heart." (7:2) When confronted with death, we are no longer dealing with side issues. We are dealing at last with realities, not negativity. Death leads to realism. Though it will bring sorrow and mourning, we set aside the shallow, ephemeral aspects of life and start to deal with the way life is. Perhaps this is why I keep finding myself drawn back to Ecclesiastes. It is a clear-eyed reminder of my mortality, of life's messiness and the absurdity of my pride. I find life shallow and wearisome when the messiness of life is ignored, when injustice and pain are whitewashed with simple platitudes.

In the face of death, Qoheleth walks the reader through the numerous vain endeavors of our world. There is no unifying topical arrangement, just a series of observations covering many areas of life. The dominant strain is figuring out how we can wrestle some order from the chaos.

In varying degrees, all people face the issues that are addressed by Ecclesiastes: lack of satisfaction or sense of purpose, financial catastrophe, personal tragedy, societal injustice, uncertainty, physical suffering, and death. Ecclesiastes challenges us to take a closer look at these important issues of life.

A prime example is the author's approach to wealth and money. Ultimately, in the face of death, wealth will be rendered useless and worthless. Any amount of money amassed, accomplishments made, or accolades won become hollow.

Through the use of paradox, Ecclesiastes points out that wealth builds and destroys, brings happiness and despair.

The message of the book of Ecclesiastes is a relevant message to people in the twenty-first century who are trapped in a world of materialism and greed. Like Qoheleth, people search for a better life but are unable to find satisfaction in the things they have.

Qoheleth recognizes that abundance and possessions lack the power to enjoy them. "Whoever loves money never has money enough; whoever loves wealth is never satisfied with his income." (5:10) "I thought in my heart, 'Come now, I will test you with pleasure to find out what is good.' But that also proved to be vanity . . . I understood great projects: I built houses and planted vineyards . . . I also possessed herds and flocks, more than anyone in Jerusalem before me. I amassed silver and gold for myself . . . I became greater by far than anyone in Jerusalem before me. Yet when I surveyed all that my hands had done and what I have toiled to achieve, everything was meaningless, a chasing after the wind." (2:1-11)

No sooner are the perils of wealth and money labeled as unimportant, than the author flips the coin over and pronounces the importance of wealth and money. His pronouncement is conditioned by an awareness of God. Because life is ultimately a gift, the opportunity to acquire wealth and money is, also, in the final analysis, a gift. "Then I realized that it is good and proper for a person to eat and drink, and to find satisfaction in toilsome labor under the sun during the few days of life God has given. Moreover, when God gives wealth and possessions, and enables us to enjoy them, to accept our lot and be happy—this is the gift of God. People seldom reflect on the days of their life, because God keeps us occupied with gladness of heart." (5:18, 19) Rather than despair, Qoheleth finds God in the midst of absurdity. Fleeting pleasures are to be enjoyed as gifts.

For the author, work that produces wealth and pleasure is viewed as both important and unimportant.

Death makes our work unimportant. "I hated life, because the work that is done under the sun, was grievous to me . . . I must leave them to the one who comes after me. And who knows whether he will be a wise man or a fool? . . . So my heart began to despair over all my toilsome labor under the sun. For people may do their work with wisdom, knowledge and skill, and then leave all they own to someone who has not worked for it." (2: 18-20)

Many people experience their work as vanity. Burnout, boredom and dissatisfaction prevail. "What do people get for all the toil and anxious striving with which they labor? . . . All work is pain and grief; even at night our mind does not rest. This also is vanity." (2:22-23)

Work becomes more rewarding when we accept the vanity side of the paradox. We will not take our work too seriously and thus worry less. Living this part of the paradox enables us to keep our work in proper perspective, thereby giving our best energy and time to other important aspects and relationships of life

Our work is very important. Those who affirm this counterpoint of the paradox find meaning and purpose in their work. Work becomes important as we acknowledge it is a gift from God. This truth makes every job valuable and important to God. When a person chooses to view his/her work as God's work, they find satisfaction. "A person can do nothing better than to eat and drink and find satisfaction in his/her work. This too, I see, is from the hand of God, for without God who can eat or find enjoyment. To the one who pleases God, God gives wisdom, knowledge and happiness." (2:24-26)

Those who understand work as a gift from God, no matter the nature of the work, experience minimal burnout and boredom. They feel satisfied because they approach their work as being God's work.

The reality of death drives the writer of Ecclesiastes to address an issue that is still relevant today. Injustice and oppression continue to present themselves in our day, especially when it comes to the issue of poverty.

"In place of justice, wickedness was there." (3:16) "If you see the poor oppressed in a district, and justice and rights denied, do not be surprised at such things; for the high official is watched by a higher, and there are yet higher ones over them."(5:8-9) Qoheleth was calling the people of that day and our day to pay attention to the injustice and oppression towards the poor.

Why should we be surprised there is poverty when we witness how profits are taken with little regard for those who are poor? Qoheleth sees prevalent injustice in the world as another example of vanity.

Some people do not see the injustice and oppression. They see poor people as lazy, content to live on government subsidies.

I wonder whether the issues surrounding poverty in 200 BCE were different from today. While the causes and solutions to poverty are varied and complex, there are still people who want to simplify the issues by categorizing poor people. Some think there is no excuse for being poor. Anyone in our country can make it if they just apply themselves. To be sure, there are lazy poor people just as there are lazy rich people. There are people who take advantage of government assistance just as there are rich people who take advantage of government assistance in the form of tax loop-holes that favor the haves and are unavailable to the have nots,.

The issues surrounding poverty include politics, education, upbringing, immigration policies, racial discrimination, economics and materialism. The writer of Ecclesiastes accurately observes that one cause of poverty is the actions and attitudes of some who have all they need. "The lover of money will not be satisfied with his income. This also is vanity." (5:10)

The issue of poverty has become a political football. People disagree on both the problem and the solution.

One side points out that more people are on welfare now than before and therefore are punishing the rich. They argue that government social programs are undermining the work ethic and creating a large class of lazy Americans who prefer to depend on government benefits rather than work. They believe government efforts to reduce poverty have failed and have actually made the problems worse. The welfare system is flawed because it rewards people for being poor, deprives them of incentives to work and undermines the family. Benefits should be linked to socially accepted behaviors such as getting a job and refraining from having more children before a family can afford it. I find this attitude about poverty to be simplistic and unrealistic.

The opposing side argues that contrary to "entitlement society" rhetoric, over nine-tenths of entitlement benefits go to the elderly, disabled or working households—not to able-bodied, working-age Americans who choose not to work. In short, both the current reality and the trends of recent decades contrast sharply with the critic's assumption that social programs increasingly are supporting people who can work but choose not to do so. At the heart of this viewpoint is the conviction that ignoring the complex issues of poverty is a threat to the economic well-being of us, as individuals and a nation. The pain that results from poverty is not the responsibility of individuals alone. We are an interdependent society and world. Therefore, the cost of addressing suffering, hunger and hopelessness of many in our nation and world should be distributed widely among us all—a goal made possible by the unique power of government to complete participation and require contributions.

By pooling the risks and resources of millions of citizens, government can guarantee that even people of limited means are able to experience the blessings of life, liberty and the pursuit of happiness. A compassionate nation and government will fulfill its purpose to "establish justice and ensure domestic tranquility . . ."

Many do not fully grasp the psychology of the poor. An intelligent conversation about poverty will include an awareness of the mental state of many poor people. Understanding the perspective of the poor is crucial. Their situation, both physically and psychologically, is very different from most of us.

Recently, I read an article entitled, "Why Can't More Poor People Escape Poverty." The article talks about how the experience of scarcity and cognitive demands affects a poor person's decision-making, particularly with respect to finances. The poor face a constant sense of urgency and in that urgency, tend to fall victim to making financial decisions that provide immediate short-term relief, but negative long-term consequences.

Without an understanding of the psychological issue of poverty, many lack empathy and consequently vilify the poor and blame them for their supposed laziness, lack of intelligence or willingness to make bad decisions. If faced with the same difficult choices, our decisions would be nearly identical. Systemic poverty in our nation will be successfully addressed through a clear understanding of the psychology of the poor.

Regardless of which position a person takes, in the midst of a world where abundance abounds, the Bible calls for humans to respond to the injustice and oppression that contributes to people suffering from poverty.

Qohleth would appreciate this story. Two turtles were talking about the world situation. One turtle said, "I wonder why God allows poverty and injustice when God could do something about it." The other turtle responded, "I think God is asking us the same question."

God is calling us to respond to the biblical concern for the poor. Power and possibilities are increased when we join our resources with others. God is calling us to join with the social services agencies in our community, stand with our church and expect our government to respond to the gap between the rich and poor.

The presence of death reminds us of the urgency of Jesus' words, "Inasmuch as you have done it to one of the least of these, you have done it to me." I invite you to join Qohleth and let thoughts of death remind us of our responsibility to live this truth of Jesus. What better way to prepare for our death.

The reality of my own death motivates me to think about the future. After I die, what is going to happen in the world? Are things going to get better or worse? I find myself both optimistic and pessimistic about the future.

When I ponder human self-centeredness, selfishness and greed, I am pessimistic. I am concerned that after I die, pain and suffering will continue and even increase as the result of poverty, prejudice and violence. I fear the possibility of a nuclear war.

At the same time, I am optimistic. God has provided and will continue to provide resources sufficient to solve the world's problems. I have hope when I see people accept their resources as a gift from God and are committed to making this a better world. I am optimistic when I see many people receive God's power and love and extend that love and power to people and places where God is working to make life filled with truth and grace.

QUESTIONS FOR CONTEMPLATION
AND DISCUSSION

1. Re-read the book of Ecclesiastes. Do you agree that this book is a positive approach to life and reality? Why? Why not?
2. Is Ecclesiastes' philosophy of eat, drink and be merry, hedonistic? Why? Why not?
3. How do you respond to Ecclesiastes' paradoxical approach to wealth, work and poverty?
4. In ways are you optimistic and pessimistic about the future?

9

MY DEATH ANXIETY
HAS DIMINISHED

I have finished my book about preparing for death. Why do I still feel my death is inconceivable? Why do I, at times, still have a horrifying feeling? Was my mission in writing this book "vanity"? Although my death anxiety is very much present, writing this book has certainly lessened it. This was one of the major reasons for my endeavors. A second reason was to help diminish your death anxiety. I hope this book has increased meaning and joy in your life as you prepare for your death with style and grace.

As you navigate down the roads of life, I strongly recommend you refer to the style as exemplified in Jesus and gratefully accept God's grace.

ORDER BOOKS

iUniverse.com
or
vbrady4216@sunflower.com
$15 (tax & postage)
Send email to schedule workshop

OTHER BOOKS BY DR. BRADY

THE SCORE IS LOVE ALL
(Timely Tips for Strong Parent/Child
Relations in Youth Sports)

BELIEVE THE BELIEVABLE
(Faith in the Face of Diversity)

KISS AND TELL
(Make Love the Married Way)